Jaja's African Hair Braiding

Jocelyn Bioh

methuen | drama

LONDON • NEW YORK • OXFORD • NEW DELHI • SYDNEY

METHUEN DRAMA

Bloomsbury Publishing Plc, 50 Bedford Square, London, WC1B 3DP, UK
Bloomsbury Publishing Inc, 1359 Broadway, New York, NY 10018, USA
Bloomsbury Publishing Ireland, 29 Earlsfort Terrace, Dublin 2,
D02 AY28, Ireland

BLOOMSBURY, METHUEN DRAMA and the Methuen
Drama logo are trademarks of Bloomsbury Publishing Plc.

First published in Great Britain 2026

Cover design: Bob King Creative

Cover image photographed by Chantel King

A catalogue record for this book is available from the British Library.

Library of Congress Control Number: 2026934407

ISBN: PB: 978-1-3506-4581-3
ePDF: 978-1-3506-4582-0
eBook: 978-1-3506-4583-7

Series: Modern Plays

Typeset by Mark Heslington Ltd, Scarborough, North Yorkshire
Printed and bound in Great Britain

For product safety related questions contact
productsafety@bloomsbury.com.

To find out more about our authors and books visit
www.bloomsbury.com and sign up for our newsletters.

This production of *Jaja's African Hair Braiding* was first performed at the Lyric Hammersmith Theatre, London on 18 March, 2026, with the following cast:

Cast (in alphabetical order)

Ndidi	**Bola Akeju**
Vanessa / Sheila / Radia	**Renee Bailey**
Aminata	**babirye bukilwa**
Jaja	**Zainab Jah**
James / Franklin / Olu / Eric	**Demmy Ladipo**
Michelle / Chrissy / LaNiece	**Dani Moseley**
Miriam	**Jadesola Odunjo**
Bea	**Dolapo Oni**
Jennifer	**Karene Peter**
Marie	**Sewa Zamba**

Creative and Production Team

Written by	**Jocelyn Bioh**
Directed by	**Monique Touko**
Set Design by	**Paul Wills**
Wigs, Hair & Make-up Design by	**Cynthia De La Rosa**
Costume Design by	**Jessica Cabassa**
Lighting Design by	**Simisola Majekodunmi**
Sound Design by	**Tony Gayle**
Video Design by	**Dick Straker**
Movement Direction by	**Kloé Dean**
Casting by	**Julia Horan CDG**
Voice & Dialect Coaches	**Joel Trill &** **Esi Acquaah-Harrison**
Associate Director	**Xanthus**
Assistant Director	**Gráinne Flynn**
Company Stage Manager	**Claire Bryan**
Deputy Stage Manager	**Sylvia Darkwa-Ohemeng**
Assistant Stage Manager	**Sarah Back**
Production Manager	**Elizabeth Dickson**

Wigs, Hair & Make-Up Supervisor	**Suzanne Scotcher**
Wigs, Hair & Make-Up Head of Department	**Teváe Humphrey**
WHAM Deputy Head of Department	**Rosemary Williams**
WHAM Assistants	**Anisa Uberoi & Isis Smith**
WHAM Artist for filming	**Niedian Biggs**
Wardrobe Assistants	**Olivia Watson & Sophia Tomlinson**
Lighting Programmer	**Stephen Settle**
Lighting Operator	**Alistair Warr**
Sound Operator	**Scott Bradley**
Video Programmer	**Grace Priest**
Video Assistant for filming	**Jakub Krumpolc**
Automation	**Tom McCreadie & Luke Mott**
Costume Supervision & Making by	**Lyric Costume Department**
Set built by	**Liverpool Scenic**
Lighting equipment supplied by	**White Light**
Video equipment supplied by	**Stage Sound Services**
Sound equipment supplied by	**Stage Sound Services**
Automation equipment supplied by	**The Revolving Stage Company & Blue Chilli Flying**
Bespoke braiding training provided by	**Levelling Up**

<u>Educators</u>
Kemi Akinbola
Teváe Humphrey
<u>Models</u>
Leah Abraham
Sabean Bea
Tashienna Bookal
Susan Browne
Ara Maydson

Braiding training support	**Angela Stewart**
Additional Set Items by	**Lyric Workshop**
Rehearsal and production photography by	**Manuel Harlan**
Poster image concept and design by	**Bob King Creative**
Poster image photography by	**Chantel King**
Programme design by	**Hannah Yates**

ABOUT THE LYRIC

The Lyric Hammersmith Theatre produces bold and relevant world-class theatre from the heart of Hammersmith, the theatre's home since 1895.

Under the leadership of Artistic Director Rachel O'Riordan and Executive Director Amy Belson, we are committed to being vital to, and representative of, our local community. A major force in London and UK theatre, the Lyric produces adventurous and acclaimed theatrical work that tells the stories that matter.

The Lyric is unique in our combined role as a local theatre serving our community, and a major national producing house with a pioneering approach to supporting young people through and into theatre. At the core of our mission and values are the people of West London, who are vital to our work as a theatre.

We are committed to working with local partners to create a cultural and creative community that brings people together, attracts visitors and supports the local economy. We bring genuinely eclectic and bold programming to West London. Our programming re-lenses familiar plays that speak directly to specific communities, and a passion to welcome and engage new audiences. The Lyric Hammersmith Theatre has a national reputation for ground-breaking work to develop and nurture the next generation of talent, providing opportunities for young people to discover the power of creativity and to experience the life changing impact of theatre.

We are the creative heart of Hammersmith, proud of our history and ambitious for our future.

Inclusion Producer
Liam Smith

Young Talent Producer
Adrian Gardner

Outreach and Partnerships Producer
Alessandra Zavagno

Young Lyric Trainee
Dominique-Nicole Sotuminu

Classes Coordinator
Ricardo Ferreira

Young Lyric Hosts
Chiquita Delisser
Ricardo Ferreira
Marisol Rojas

DEVELOPMENT TEAM

Director of Development
Zosha Nash

Head of Individual Giving
Lina Stein

Development Manager
Francesca Mirabile

COMMUNICATIONS & SALES TEAM

Director of Communications and Sales
Grace Organ

Senior Marketing Manager
Millie Whittam

Marketing Manager
Hannah McLelland

Sales and Box Office Manager
Robin Wilks

Press & Marketing Assistant
Mutiat Akamo

BOX OFFICE ASSISTANT (PART-TIME)

Chanel Fernandes
Kailas Sreekumar

BOX OFFICE ASSISTANTS (CASUAL)

Charlotte Kiely
Ellie Bibby
Emer Halton-O'Mahony
Farshid Rokey
Genevieve Sabherwal
James Douglas-
Quarcoopome

lydia luke
Mackenzie Larsen
Mara Simão
Talia Kracauer
Sophia Rasab
Dana Gough
Beth Calvert-Lee

FINANCE & RESOURCES TEAM

Director of Finance & Resources
Wendy Dempsey

Financial Controller
Charlotte Lines

Accounts and Payroll Co-Ordinator
Lesley Williams

Finance Officer
Kunle Sanni

HR Business Partner
Beverley Dash

Administration Manager
Meghana Shah

Head of Building & Facilities
Brian Elvins

Facilities Manager
Hannah Victory

Maintenance Assistant
Laurie Foster

Security Supervisor
Jean-Baptiste Maizeroi

Duty Security
David Kalloo
Sam Thompson

Housekeeping Team
Bright Gyau
Feni Wilson
Abdul-Hak Laaraj
Dipesh Sinchuri

Ivan Velinov
Nnamdi Ernest Ugorji
Onisofe Isaac

PRODUCTION TEAM

Head of Production
Seamus Benson

Company Stage Manager
Claire Bryan

Deputy Head of Production
Elizabeth Dickson

Head of Lighting
Dan Miller

Head of Sound & Video
Daniel Ronayne

Head of Costume
Hannah Gilbert

Studio & Events Technical Manager
George Ogilvie

Stage Deputy
Tom McCreadie

Sound Deputy
Scott Bradley

COMMERCIAL TEAM

Commercial Director
Paul Gallagher

Bars & Catering Manager
Gareth Chalmers

Events and Hires Manager
Tim Jones

Head Bars & Catering Supervisor
Viktor Velkovski

Hires & Bookings Assistant
Ashley Quagraine-McVay

Visitor Experience Manager
Luke Vogel

Senior Duty Manager
Stephanie Dawes

Casual Duty Managers
Hana Jennings
Annie Howlett
Raquel Taveira-Marques

Visitor Experience Supervisors
Ellie Bibby
Wesley Bozonga
Beth Calvert Lee
Mackenzie Larsen
Ashley Quagraine-McVay
Emma Price
Jack Dickson
Joshua Bendall
Ez Scarborough

Visitor Experience Assistants
James Barlow
Thusika Baskaran
Hebe Cooke
Matthew Cowan
Amelia Cramer
Hannah Crosby
Ren Edwards
Syeda Fatima
Isabella Forshaw
Laura González Urueta
Anoushka Hem
Stephan Hunte-Wilson
Katie Hutchings
Prime Isaac
Deborah Jardine
Veronica Jegede

Madison Wells Live

Founded by producer Gigi Pritzker, Madison Wells is an award-winning independent entertainment company that empowers badass women and boundary-pushing storytellers. Its projects span acclaimed films and television, including the Oscar-winning *The Eyes of Tammy Faye*; Netflix's #1 global hit Nonnas; Sundance Audience Award-winner *Prime Minister*; the Sundance Short Film Grand Jury Prize-winning *The Baddest Speechwriter of All* (acquired by Netflix); and National Geographic's anthology series *Genius*. Madison Wells' live entertainment arm has built a curated slate of stage productions devoted to essential, artist-driven storytelling. Select theatre credits include *Hadestown* (Tony Award for Best Musical); *Swept Away*; *Jaja's African Hair Braiding* (Tony nomination for Best Play); *Company* (Tony Award for Best Revival of a Musical); *The Inheritance* (Tony Award for Best Play); *Hold On to Me Darling*; and *The Ocean at the End of the Lane* (Olivier nomination for Best Play), among others on Broadway, Off-Broadway, and the West End. Madison Wells also partners with like-minded entertainment companies—including two-time Academy Award-winning Breakwater Studios, chart-topping audio company Lemonada Media, and global streaming platform Mubi—that share its belief that great storytelling can provoke, inspire, and move audiences around the world.

www.madisonwellsmedia.com

Chase This Productions

CHASE THIS PRODUCTIONS was founded in 2024 by Jessica Chase, an independent producer and creative consultant working across theater, television, and film. Previous productions include the World Premiere of pre-existing condition by Marin Ireland and the US Premiere of *Strategic Love Play* by Miriam Battye. Previously for Broadway she served on the Lead Producing Team of *Life of Pi*, the Co-producing teams of *POTUS; Or Behind Every Great Dumbass Are Seven Women Trying to Keep Him Alive*, and *The Piano Lesson*. She produced the UK Debut of Jocelyn Bioh's *School Girls; Or, The African Mean Girls Play* with The Lyric Hammersmith, Francesca Moody Productions, and Idris Elba. Before that Jessica was the Artistic Producer of MCC Theater where she worked from 2011 until 2020, overseeing the development of new work, programming, and production.

www.chasethisproductions.com

Jaja's African Hair Braiding

Characters

Jaja, *forties-plus; Senegalese; owner of the shop. The backbone and/or saving grace of everyone in the shop. Getting married today in City Hall to Steven—the landlord of a local building.*
Marie, *eighteen; Jaja's daughter who runs the shop for her mother; has a lot of weight on her young shoulders because of her circumstances. Secretly wants to be a writer; has a fun and silly side, but is firm and assertive when needed—especially with the women in the shop.*
Bea *(pronounced Bee), forties; Ghanaian; has been at the shop the longest; the neighborhood gossip with an unpredictable attitude— she seems addicted to causing drama, but is rarely ever wrong.*
Miriam, *early to mid-twenties; Sierra Leonean; very kind and seemingly quiet on the surface, but has a fierce spirit underneath her shell; loves the idea of love and is the epitome of an optimist.*
Aminata, *thirties; Senegalese; fun, sexy and charming. She loves her job and is good at it, but also loves to hang out at the shop as well. The shop is both her job and her favorite place to be social. Has a tumultuous and passionate marriage; Bea's sidekick in gossip and drama when necessary.*
Ndidi *(pronounced In-dee-dee), late twenties/early thirties; Nigerian; the young spitfire; she dresses the youngest and braids the fastest. Everyone at the shop knows that she makes the most money and that doesn't always go over well with everyone—namely Bea.*
Jennifer, *twenties; Black American; aspiring journalist; comes to the shop wanting to get micro braids and is in the shop all day; incredibly patient and caring.*

Vanessa/Sheila/Radia

Vanessa, *thirties; super-rude customer that no one wants to deal with.*
Sheila, *thirties; the friendly but loud-talking businesswoman. She enjoys a little gossip like the next person.*
Radia *(pronounced like Nadia), eighteen-ish; one of Marie's former classmates.*

Michelle/Chrissy/Laniece

Michelle, *twenties; The nervous client who doesn't want trouble and just wants to get her hair done peacefully.*
Chrissy, *thirties; really wants braids that will "make her look like Beyoncé".*
Laniece, *twenties; a regular at the shop; works as a DJ so she always gets funky braid styles. She likes to have a good time and loves a good meal.*

James/Franklin, The Sock Man/Olu, The Jewelry Man/Eric, The DVD Man

James, *thirties; Ghanaian; Aminata's on-again, off-again husband who clearly takes advantage of her.*
Franklin, The Sock Man, *thirties; quick-talking and friendly neighborhood salesman just trying to make a living; Black American.*
Olu, The Jewelry Man, *thirties; a shy, honest man just trying to make a living; has a bit of a crush on Ndidi; Nigerian.*
Eric, The DVD Man, *thirties; the caring DVD man who looks out for his friends; Senegalese.*

Note: All characters are of Black American and/or West African Descent and are to be played by Black actors.

Setting

A hair-braiding shop in Harlem off of 125th Street.

Time

A very hot day in July of 2019.

Playwright's Note

For most of my life, truly since I was four years old, I have been wearing my hair in braids. I have had braids for so long, I can actually name the three times in my life when I did *not* have braids or some type of extensions for a significant amount of time. So I have spent a very large portion of my life in hair-braiding shops and can tell you all about them. The stuffy ones that have way too many braiders in too small of a room. The shop that only has one hair braider because she likes her peace of mind. The shop that is located behind another place of business (a barber shop, a bodega, a pharmacy, a fish market—I've seen it all). I've gone to 125th street and taken my chance with the kind hair-braiding lady standing on the corner, flagging down any customer she could find; always with the standard sales pitch: "Hair braiding, miss?" I'm always arrested by the relief on their faces when someone responds, "Yes, I'd like to get my hair braided." I imagine that at least for the next few hours, their dignity is restored. This play is for each and every person who enters the shop. Their hopes. Their dreams. Their incredible stories of how and why they came to this country. I celebrate these amazing women and thank them for what they do. To many people, they are just "hair-braiding ladies," random women people pass by on the street, but to me they are heroes, craftswomen, and artists with beautiful, gifted, and skilled hands.

Dedicated to all of my favorite hair-braiding ladies: Auntie Maggie, Auntie Cassandra, my sister Jackie, Ali Berry, the sisters—Salimatou and Jaja, Sira in LA, and my current miracle worker—Nafi. Thank you for saving my life and my hair.

And to all the dreamers and my dear best friend, Tolu—I love you beyond words.

Scene One: 9am

It's a quiet and hot summer morning on 125th and St. Nicholas Avenue in Harlem. **Miriam** *is drinking a smoothie and waiting in front of a closed "Jaja's African Hair Braiding" shop. After a moment,* **Marie** *runs up. She is carrying a bunch of "Ghana Must Go" bags that are very heavy. She plops them down in front of the grate.*

Miriam   Good morning.

Marie   Hi. Good morning. Sorry. So sorry.

Marie   I hope you weren't waiting long.   **Miriam**   No, no, it's fine. I wasn't waiting long.

Marie *fumbles to get the keys out of her large bookbag. She goes through the process of unlocking the grate and opening up the shop all while speaking.*

Marie   It's just been one of those days already you know? I slept through my alarm, which like, I don't even know how. That never happens to me. Then the hot water wasn't running in our building—and like, I know it's hot today, but not hot enough to just be taking a freezing cold shower— which I had to anyways.

Then I threw on my clothes and ran out of the house. I get to the station, swipe my Metrocard and, of course— "Insufficient Fare"—UGH!

But it was actually a good thing because I realized that I forgot to bring the new packs of hair that FINALLY came in after all of this back and forth with the post office and you know how much fun that is for me! Even though cute Johnny has been working the morning shifts, but anyway, anyway.

I'm just not tryna deal with all of the braiders coming down on me today about not having enough new hair for the week, mainly, my mother—because you know that I would never hear the end of it from her.

(*Imitates her mother.*) "Eh-eh! So you want me to go broke?! Be starving in the streets? You want to ruin my business and my shop?! Hmph! I know you are my daughter, but darling, I will not let aaaaaaaanyone ruin my business while God is still keeping me alive! You understand?"

Miriam   You sound just like Jaja.

She laughs both amused at **Marie***'s spot-on impersonation of her mother and the glaring accuracy of her words.* **Marie** *prattles on while continuing this intricate choreography of unlocking the grate and pushing it up. It feels like a big job for such a tiny girl, but* **Marie** *is used to this dance.*

Marie   But you know what I mean. Anyway, I go back home, grab the bags, run back to the train station, refill my Metrocard, and catch an A train right as it pulls in.

But then it's like . . . Okay, is this an express train or what?!

Like whhhhhhhyyyy does it move so slow? There's train traffic every day? Every minute? How? But whatever, I finally made it! Anyways . . . Hi! How was your morning?

Miriam   Fine.

Marie *and* **Miriam** *finally enter the stuffy shop.*

Marie   God—It's going to be a hot one today.

Miriam   Yeah, I saw on the news it's going to be close to 100.

Marie   Well, hopefully it doesn't get too packed in here.

(*Speaking to the air conditioner.*) I need you to stay working today, okay little air conditioner?

Miriam *notices a notebook that* **Marie** *placed on the front counter along with her things.*

Miriam (*reading the title*)   "For the love I lost in the sea" by Marie Ndiaye (en-de-EYE). Your new short story?

Marie *nods—shy but proud.*

Marie   Yeah . . .

Miriam   Okay! So what is this one about?

Marie   Okay, so boom: it's about two people, from the Caribbean, but from two different classes, and they meet on a boat and fall in love, but lose touch once they reach America.

Miriam (*a little confused*)   Like *Titanic*?

Marie   Yes. Well, no. I mean . . . there are similarities I guess.

(*Immediately worried.*)   Oh no . . . I actually never thought about that comparison.

Miriam   Hey—Black *Titanic* love story sound good to me.

Marie   Sure, but this one is deeper. More romantic. I think you'd like this one a lot.

Miriam   Well, me, you know I like reading all of your stories. I think it help me make my English better.

Marie   Aww thanks, Miriam.

Miriam   Eh heh. So now, this your third one. And you still don't want to tell your mom you want to be a writer and not doctor like she want?

Marie   You know that she doesn't understand. If it's not a job that screams "I make a lot of money," then it's pointless to her. So I can't tell her I want to write for a living.

Miriam   But your mom like romance story. Look, she's getting married today!

Marie (*sarcasm*)   I wouldn't call that romance, Miriam.

Miriam   Ah, Marie, don't say that.

Marie   It's true.

Miriam   Anyway, are you hungry? Would you like this bagel?

Marie   Oh, thank you. You're the best. I didn't get a chance to grab breakfast.

Miriam   It's no problem. I got the special at my new corner deli and it comes with bagel. But you know me, I'm trying to watch my weight.

Marie   What are you talking about? You look amazing.

Miriam   No, no. I saw CNN doctor say that if you want to lose weight, you have to not have too many "carbs."

Marie   So you're never going to eat bread again?

Miriam   Not forever but, I am going back home in two months and I don't want my family to say anything. And they are *always* saying something.

Marie   Mmm hmmm . . . And do these sudden weight goals have anything to do with Musa?

Miriam (*feigned surprise*)   What? No. I am not even thinking about him.

Marie   So it's just a funny coincidence that your friend who came in the other day told you that he was single and now all of a sudden, bread is the devil?

Miriam   She was just catching me up!

Marie   You literally screamed and jumped up and down.

Miriam   It's exciting to hear about old friends from back home in Sierra Leone. This is not about Musa. This is about carbs.

Marie   Okay. Well you know that includes rice, right?

Miriam (*looks completely shocked*)   WHAT?

Aminata *enters the shop. She's out of breath already from the heat.*

Aminata   *Bonjour.*

Miriam   *Ca va.*

Marie   Good morning, Aminata. How are you?

Aminata (*sucks her teeth*)   Ah, is the air con on? It's hot, o!

Miriam   She just turned it on.   **Marie**   I just turned it on. It's going to take a while to cool.

Aminata *plops her bag down at her station and sits in her chair.*

Aminata   Marie, please. Can you bring me some water? I need to take my pill.

Marie *pours a cup of water from the cooler.*

Aminata   These doctors.

(*Sucks teeth.*) Telling me that my blood pressure is high. For what? How do you know?

Marie   Well, did they run tests?

Aminata   Yeah. And it was high. Then he said that I should try to eat less salt, get more sleep and "relax." That I have too much stress.

Miriam   Oh, I'm sorry, sista.

Aminata   Of course I have stress! You are telling me I have high blood pressure and that I'm going to die!

Bea   Ah-ah! Who is dying?

Bea *walks into the shop.*

Marie   No one.

Bea   Why is it so hot? Is the   **Aminata**   We just put it on.
air conditioner broken?

Marie (*eating*)   It'll cool down soon.

Bea (*playful*)   Oh so you don't bring a bagel for me?

Marie   I didn't buy this. Miriam gave it to me.

Bea   I thought you gave up bread?

Miriam   I did. That's why she's eating it.

Bea (*shaking her head*)   Miriam. You are not taking this serious. I'm telling you.

Miriam   I am. Trust me, I am.

Aminata *turns on the television. She tries to search for what she wants to watch.*

Aminata   Marie, how do you put on the YouTube again? (*Sucks teeth.*) These smart TVs. How smart are they, eh?

Aminata   Me, I don't understand them.   **Bea**   My son just bought me one. It's so good.

Marie *takes the remote from* **Aminata**.

Marie   What do you want to watch?

Bea   Ah-ah, no Nollywood yet, eh? It's too early. I don't want to hear all of that shouting.

Aminata   Put on that music station. You know? With the song that I like by that one guy?

Marie (*she doesn't know*)   Uh . . .

Aminata   Ah, Marie. You know the song. You were just singing it.   **Bea**   Just yesterday you were singing it.

Marie   I never sing anything.

Aminata   You know the song. It's like—

Aminata *and* **Bea** *both mumble sing something that is not distinct.*

Aminata   You know?

Bea   If you play it, we'll know it.

Aminata   Yeah.

Marie *is unsure. She puts on a YouTube station that plays an Afrobeat song. (If you can get the rights, perhaps "On the Low" by Burna Boy.)* **Aminata** *starts dancing to it.*

Marie   Is that it?

Aminata   No, but leave it on. I like it.

Jennifer *enters the shop.*

Marie   Good morning. Can I help you?

Jennifer   Hi. Do you all take walk-ins?

Bea *makes a show of dusting off her chair.*

Bea   Yeah. What style you want?

Jennifer   Oh, um. Just like long braids.

Bea   Box braids.

Jennifer   Yeah. My friend comes here and she said you guys do a good job.

Bea   Of course. We do it nice-nice for you.

Jennifer   Thank you.

Bea   How big you want it?

Jennifer   Umm not too big.

Bea   Medium?

Jennifer   No, I was thinking micros actually.

Bea   Oh.

Bea's *friendly demeanor ceases.* **Aminata** *and* **Marie** *try to hold back their laughter.*

Bea   Uhh, here. My friend Miriam. She will do it for you.

(*Shouts.*) Miriam! She said she wants micros.

Miriam (*trying to look excited*)   Oh. Okay.

Jennifer   Y'all got the hair, right?

Marie   Yes, we have everything here.

Jennifer   Okay, and how much is it?

Miriam   Come.

She walks towards the front door and **Jennifer** *looks confused.*

Marie (*to* **Jennifer**)   She'll talk to you about the price outside.

Jennifer   Oh. I thought I was getting kicked out.

Marie   No, no. Not at all.

Jennifer *follows* **Miriam** *out.*

Bea   No, you are just getting kicked out of my chair.

Aminata (*laughs*)   So you don't want to make money, eh?

Bea   Listen, I am not breaking my fingers today. Long micro braids? She is going to be in here all day.

Aminata   It's fine. Miriam is fast.

Bea   Sha! No one is that fast.

Aminata *busies herself with going through her stack of scratch-off lottery tickets.*

Aminata (*to the scratch-offs*)   Come on. Let me get lucky today, eh! I want a new designer handbag.

Bea   You know no one ever wins those things. You're wasting your time.

Aminata   You didn't see that lady who won on the news yesterday? Twenty thousand dollars. Can you imagine?!

The shop phone rings. **Marie** *answers it.*

Marie   Jaja's African Hair Braiding . . . Mommy, hi . . . Yes, I brought all of the hair . . . Yes, even the box in the back closet   No I'm about to separate it now . . . I will . . . No problem. Yes. Okay. Bye.

Bea *and* **Aminata** *look at* **Marie** *curiously.*

Bea   So your mother is not coming in today?

Marie (*avoiding*)   Ummm, I'm not sure actually.

Aminata   Oh, I'm surprised she doesn't want to come in and show off on her wedding day.

Marie   Yeah. Anyway, I'm going to the back to start sorting out the packs if anyone needs me.

Aminata   Okay.

Marie *heads to the back room.* **Bea** *and* **Aminata** *seize on this time to gossip—their favorite activity.*

Bea   Heh! Jaja and her white man! You can't tell her anything.

Aminata   Did she show you pictures of her dress?

Bea   That "custom-made" ugly thing?

Aminata   It was not that bad.

Bea   It's hideous. It looks like she took a bag of, eh, eh, what are those things—marshmallows and just cha-cha them together to make a dress.

Aminata   Listen, maybe that's what (*mocks his name*) *Steven* wants.

Bea (*mocking* **Jaja**)   "Oh me and *Steven* are going to buy an apartment downtown. We are looking at places."

Aminata (*continues to mock*)   "*Steven* took me to a Broadway show. It was so nice."

Bea   "*Steven* has some great ideas for how to make the shop better. Just wait! This is going to be the best shop in Harlem."

Aminata   Well, today is it. She's finally going to get married and get her papers.

Bea   Oh please! How can she marry a man who is already with someone else?

Aminata   What do you mean?

Bea   I told you, my friend Akua lives in the building next door to his. Steven is her super too and she says that she always sees him with this lady. And that he takes out her trash and brings in her groceries. She even said that she saw them kiss like right here. On the street. In broad daylight.

(*Points to the corner of her mouth.*) I'm telling you. Jaja is fooling herself. He is cheating on her!

Miriam *and* **Jennifer** *walk back into the shop.*

Miriam   Okay, well have a seat in that chair. Let me get the hair ready for you.

Jennifer   Thank you.

Miriam (*to* **Aminata**)   Is Marie in the back?

Aminata (*she knows*)   I don't know.

Miriam (*calls out*)   Marie? I need number 2 in 28 inches. Bring out a lot of packs please.

Marie (*offstage*)   Okay. Coming.

Ndidi   Morning!

Ndidi *walks into the shop. She is jamming out to the music on her headphones.*

Aminata (*sucks teeth*)   This one here.

Miriam   Morning, Ndidi. How are you?

Ndidi *doesn't respond as her music is too loud.*

Bea   Look at her. Just rude.

Miriam *waves to get* **Ndidi**'s *attention.*

Miriam   Good morning.

Ndidi (*takes off headphones*)   Oh hi, sorry. I was into my song.

Miriam   It's fine. How are you?

Ndidi   I'm good. Eh, I like this dress. Very nice, o!

Miriam (*flattered*)   Oh, thank you.

Aminata (*sucks teeth*)   This girl.

Bea (*a little too loud*)   Hmph!

Ndidi   Good morning, ladies.

Aminata Hi . . .   **Bea**   Mmmm . . .

Ndidi   How are you doing today?

Aminata   Fine.

Bea   I'm good.

Ndidi   Great.

She starts to prep her station for her first customer. **Marie** *brings out large packs of hair for* **Miriam**.

Marie   Here you go.

Miriam   Thank you.

(*To* **Jennifer**.) This is the color that you want right?

Jennifer   Yup, that's it. Thank you.

Miriam   Okay, good.

She starts to comb **Jennifer**'*s hair, but* **Jennifer** *winces.*

Jennifer   Umm, can you comb lightly please. I'm kinda tender-headed.

Miriam   Okay. No problem.

Bea (*talking to* **Aminata** *about* **Ndidi**)   Can you believe this one? Talking to me like we're friends.

Aminata   Don't worry about this girl. She's just silly.

Bea   I'm telling you! And you see how she's all "Good morning!" like she's nice. We know she's not nice.

Aminata   I know.

Bea (*sucks teeth*)   Anyway . . . I'm not going to let her mess with me today. I'm not.

Marie   Going to pick up some water. Does anyone want anything from the deli?

Miriam (*takes a sip of her smoothie*)   No, I'm fine.

Bea   Egg sandwich and ginger tea.

Aminata   Onion bagel with cream cheese.

Ndidi   Bacon, egg, and cheese on a roll.

Marie   Cool. Alright, I'll be back.

She exits.

Bea (*to* **Aminata**—*sucks teeth*)   Bacon, egg, and cheese. You see how she copies me? I get an egg sandwich and then she wants the same thing with bacon and cheese. You see this nonsense?

Aminata   Yeah I see it.

Bea   Ehhhh-verything I do, this girl wants it. It's crazy.

Aminata   I know.

Ndidi *takes off her headphones. Clearly there was no music playing this time.*

Ndidi   Sista Bea . . . Is there a problem? Today? Again?

Bea   Excuse me?

Ndidi   You know I can hear you.

Bea   Okay. So you say what?

Ndidi   No YOU say what?

Bea   Eh-eh! Who are you pointing at?

Miriam   Ladies.

Ndidi   Listen, I don't want any problems with you. I just want to do my job and go home. That's it.

Bea   Me too.

Ndidi   Good. Great!

It should be over, but **Bea** *likes to start shit.*

Bea   —And if you don't steal any more of my customers, we won't have any problems.

Ndidi   Are you serious?

Bea   Eh-eh! Natasha has been coming to me for YEARS. And then all of a sudden, I walk in and she's sitting in your chair. How is that not stealing?

(*To* **Aminata**.) Aminata. Is that not stealing?

Aminata   Sounds like stealing to me.

Ndidi   Oh so I forced her? She called ME, okay?

Bea   And how did she get your number?

Ndidi   I don't know! From her friend who recommended me.

Aminata (*laughs*)   "Recommended." Hmph! By who?

Bea   Exactly.

Ndidi   Look, I'm not doing background checks on every customer who calls me. I'm sorry about Natasha. But I'm not doing this back and forth with you everyday while I'm here. As soon as they are done renovating my shop, I'm gone.

Bea   That's right. Your chair   **Aminata**   Temporary!
is temporary. If your shop hadn't
burned down and Jaja didn't feel
sorry for you, you wouldn't even
be here. So mind yourself, yeah?
You should be grateful.

Aminata   Grateful!

Ndidi   I am.

Bea   Then act like it.

Aminata   Yeah!

Ndidi *laughs and shakes her head as she puts on her headphones and plays her music loud again.*

Bea   You see? That's why she put on her headphones. Because she knows I'm right! . . . Anyway . . . What were we even talking about?

Aminata   Jaja's wedding.

Bea   Oh right. That sham marriage.

Aminata   Eh! Bea!

Bea   Listen, I wish Jaja would just stop lying and call it what it is, yeah? When I married stupid Peter from my church, you think I was in love with him?

They laugh.

No! Who could love a man that hideous? But he needed his papers and he offered me a good price.

Aminata   Do you still even talk to him?

Bea   No. For what? After the divorce, I didn't care! And that's exactly what Steven is going to say to Jaja!

Aminata   Aye! Bea. Come now.

Bea   I'm telling you. I give it two months. He's going to drop her fast-fast and she will be right back in this shop, breaking her fingers, braiding hair all day, trying to make ends meet like the rest of us.

You see—that is her problem: She's always wanted too much, too soon. She thinks she's better than everyone.

Ndidi *scoffs and chuckles to herself, but* **Bea** *is too self-involved to notice.*

Bea   You know this whole plan for a shop? This was my idea.

Aminata *(really everyone) has heard this story* many *times before.*

Aminata   Oh yes. I remember.

Bea   The concept, the design, how to run it, everything. It was all my idea and she stole it from me.

Miriam   Bea—Are we still on this?

Bea   It's true!

Miriam *(rolls her eyes)*   Okay.

Bea   Everyone knows that! Back in the day, hmm—me and Jaja were like this.

(She crosses her fingers.) We would be cleaning these white people's houses and would talk all the time about the shop that we were going to open. Where it would be, how much money we would make, everything. And then she met that sleazy landlord who offered "a deal she couldn't pass up" she said.

Sucks teeth.

I told her not to use all the money she had saved for an immigration lawyer on this. I said that getting her Green Card was more important, but she was determined . . .

And because I couldn't get all of my money together in time, she went ahead. Hmph. I'm telling you—this place should be called Bea's African Hair Braiding!

Marie *enters.* **Bea** *changes her tone.*

Bea   But, anyway, it's fine. As soon as I have my money sorted, I will get a nice property, on a nice block, and open my own shop. The *right* way.

Ndidi *rolls her eyes.*

Aminata   You've been saying this for years now, Bea.

Bea   Eh-eh! You don't know business, Ami. These things take time.

Aminata   Sure.

Marie (*handing out orders*)   Alright, here's your sandwich, Bea.

Bea   Thank you.

Marie   And for you, Aminata.

Aminata   Thanks.

Marie   And you got the bacon, egg, and cheese, right, Ndidi?

Bea *sucks her teeth and rolls her eyes.*

Ndidi   Yes. Thank you.

Marie   No problem.

Miriam (*to* **Jennifer**)   How is it? Are you feeling okay?

Jennifer   Yup. I'm good. Thank you. I know this is going to take a while, so I'm just trying to get comfortable.

Miriam   I know. But I will try to do it fast-fast for you, eh?

Jennifer   Thanks.

The air conditioner makes a scary sound. Has it broken? Oh God. Not today. Everyone starts fanning themselves.

Everyone   Ah-ah! / Now what is going on here? / Is it broken? / Oh my goodness.

Bea   This thing is trying to kill us!

Aminata   It's too hot for this.

Miriam   I think you need to come and fix the air con, Marie.

Everyone   Eh heh! / 'Cause it's too much. / Eh, this heat. / I'm dying, oh.

Marie   Sorry y'all. I think it's just going to be one of those days.

Everyone   Ughhhhh!

Marie *starts clicking things on the air conditioner remote—hoping it will fix it.*

Scene Two: 12pm

A music video from the YouTube channel continues to play on the TV. (If you can get the rights, perhaps "Eminado" by Tiwa Savage feat. Don Jazzy.) The shop is a bit more busy now although **Bea** *and* **Aminata** *do not have a customer in their chairs yet.* **Miriam** *is still working on* **Jennifer***'s hair and, though minimal, she's made progress.* **Ndidi** *is finishing the long cornrow style of a new customer,* **Chrissy.** **Marie** *is sweeping up the shop.* **Aminata** *is dancing around and not doing much work.*

Bea   So this is not the song?

Aminata   No. I'm telling you. I'll know it when I hear it. But I like this one, now. It's good.

Bea   This girl. She does more dancing than braiding.

They all laugh.

Aminata   Excuse me? This is how I get my exercise in.

They all encourage **Aminata** *as she gets down one last time before her cell phone starts to ring. All the joy she had drops away as she sees who is calling her.*

(*Into phone.*) What did I tell you, James? I'm not talking to you. Stop calling my phone before I block you, eh?!

(*Listens.*) No! I don't want to hear it. I'm tired of it and I'm tired of you!

She hangs up. **Bea** *gives her a knowing look.*

Bea   Why don't you just divorce that man?

Aminata   It's not that easy, Bea.

Bea   This is America—trust me—yes it is.

Aminata   I know he will change. It's just taking some time.

Bea   Five years is a lot of time.

Aminata   I don't want to talk about it now, okay?

Bea   Fine. But I would not be a good friend if I didn't tell you the truth, Ami.

The music on the TV is interrupted by a commercial ad:

Television Ad   Somewhere inside each of us is a calling. Whether it's to be a doctor, a lawyer, an engineer, or a teacher. What are you being called to do? Discover it here at Borough of Manhattan Community College.

The ad makes **Marie** *stop. She stares at the TV for a moment and then tries to continue sweeping.*

Miriam   Eh! Isn't that your school, Marie?

Marie   Umm, the one my mom has a "connect" for, yeah.

Miriam   Did you tell her you don't want to go?

Marie   I've tried to a bunch of times, but you know how she is.

Bea   Hmph . . . I know it well.

Miriam   Ah, but I think you're right about waiting to see if you can do an Ivy League school. You never know what can happen in a year.

Marie   She thinks that her and Steven getting married will fix everything and . . . it's just not that simple.

Bea   Exactly! Listen—I told her. I said that she should have handled this when you all first came. I even knew a guy— offering a good deal for marriage papers—would only charge seven thousand. Hey! A steal—you hear me? I paid at least ten for mine.

Miriam   I think Marie is saying she wants to do things her way and not how Jaja like to do things.

Aminata   Please, America is just like back home.

Ndidi   They just hide it better.

Aminata   They solve anything with money.

Ndidi   It's all just about who you know.

Aminata   Eh heh!

Bea   Look at those white people whose house your mother was cleaning. If they were not on the board of your school, how else do you think you would have been able to go there?

Marie *looks at* **Bea** *with the "can you not put my business in the street" face.*

Marie   Okay . . .

Miriam   Bea, come on.

Bea   What? Everyone knows that's how Marie got into that fancy school.

Miriam   Yes, but she took test and got highest scores at the school. She earned it.

Marie   It's fine. Miriam.

Bea   All I'm saying is that Jaja puts too much faith in these white people. Okay, so they helped Marie that time. Fine. But when Jaja went to them asking if they would help with her papers, all of a sudden it was, "Oh, we don't know. We don't feel comfortable." And now look? She's still stuck.

Aminata   Not after today.

Bea   Sure. Okay. And when Marie wants to go to Princeton or Columbia, whose house is Jaja going to clean then?

Aminata   Eh, Bea!

No one has a real response. **Marie** *is mortified.*

Bea   Exactly!

Marie   Can we just—

Miriam   —But what about the Dreams thing? What is it?

Bea   Dooka. Decca. Something like that.

Miriam   What Obama signed.

Marie   DACA?

Aminata   The Dream Act.

Miriam   Yeah, that's it.

Bea   Yeah, DECCA. That's what I said. I saw it on the news.

Marie (*sighs*)   It's crazy expensive actually. And really not easy to—

Miriam   —How much? Maybe we can all give you the money—

All Women   —Eh heh! / Yes! / How much do you need?

Marie (*cutting everyone off*)   —You know, I really don't wanna talk about ANY of this anymore, okay?! I don't want to talk about school or my mother or her "connections" or whatever you saw on the news! Trust me—this is already all I think about every single day. Every single second! For once, can I just have a day where I come here, do my work—in peace—and go home? Is that okay?!

Beat. The shop falls silent. **Aminata** *and* **Bea** *make eyes at each other.* **Miriam** *smiles solemnly at* **Marie**.

Miriam (*to* **Marie**)   Listen, God will work it out for you, eh? You will see. God can make anything happen in your life.

All Women   Amen! / Yes, praise God! / He will work it out for you.

Franklin, The Sock Man *enters the shop. He pulls in his large shopping cart and display of different colored/designed socks.*

The Sock Man   What's going on y'all. What's going on?

All Women   Good afternoon / How are you? / Hello / Hi, Franklin.

The Sock Man   Socks. Socks. I got socks. I got socks. Long ones. Short ones. Winter socks. Summer socks. Color socks. Black socks. White socks. Whatever socks you want. Trust me, I got. Socks. Socks. Socks.

Anyone need socks?

Jennifer   Ooh, can I see?

The Sock Man   Sure. Got a bunch right here. And much more in my cart.

Jennifer   How much are these?

The Sock Man   What you wanna pay, sis? I'll give you a good price.

Chrissy (*holding up a picture on her phone to show* **Ndidi**)   You know, it's funny because people tell me I look like Beyoncé all the time, but with my hair like this, I like really see it.

Ndidi   Yeah . . .

Chrissy   And can you see about braiding it all the way to the end like this?

Ndidi   Okay. No problem.

Chrissy   'Cause this is for my birthday party and I need my hair to look exactly like how hers did in the video.

Ndidi   I understand.

Chrissy (*looking in the mirror*)   See. Sorry. I don't want to be picky or whatever, but this braid right here doesn't have enough blonde.

Ndidi   Okay, I'll redo it.

Chrissy   Yeah, 'cause I need it to look EXACT. You know what I'm saying?

Ndidi   No problem. I will make you Beyoncé today.

Chrissy   Thank you.

Jennifer   Okay, let me get these two and then three pairs of these black ones.

The Sock Man   No problem, miss, no problem. I'll give you all of these for twenty.

Jennifer   Okay, I love a good deal. Thank you.

Jennifer *hands him some money.*

The Sock Man   No, no, thank you. (*To* **Chrissy**.) And for you: Miss Beyoncé. You need socks?

Chrissy (*flattered*)   Oh my God. You are so stupid. But nah, I'm not Beyoncé. And I'm good on socks right now.

The Sock Man   No problem, miss. Next time. Hey, Marie. Tell your mother I said hello and congratulations.

Marie   I will. See you, Franklin.

He holds the door open for a new customer walking in, **Vanessa**. *She doesn't thank him. Everything about how she's walked in suggests that she's . . . not the most fun person in the world (aka: rude).*

The Sock Man (*as he exits*)   Socks. Socks. Socks. I got socks for sale. Socks.

Marie   Hello. Welcome. How can I help you?

Vanessa   Yeah. I wanna get braids.

Marie   Okay great. Do you know what style you want?

Vanessa   No. Y'all don't got a book or somethin'?

Marie   Uh, yeah we do.

(*Pulls a photo album from behind the counter.*) Here you go.

Vanessa   Ummm, this is like dumb heavy. You wanna break my arm?

Marie   Oh. No, sorry.

Vanessa   I like just got my nails done and shit.

Marie   Sorry.

Aminata *and* **Bea** *look at each other and shake their heads. Beat.* **Vanessa** *looks through the album quickly.*

Marie   Uh . . . do you know what kind of style you'd like?

Vanessa   Damn! I literally just said I ain't know! Like . . . chill.

Marie   Sorry, I was just trying to help.

Vanessa   Well, when I need help, I'm a ask, aight?

Marie   Sure.

Vanessa (*shows* **Marie**)   Aight, so I want this.

Marie   Great. Jumbo box braids.

Vanessa   Yeah. How much is that?

Marie (*looks around*)   Well . . . Let me see who's avail . . .able . . .

Marie *looks over to all of the braiders in the shop and* **Aminata** *and* **Bea** *do a poor job of looking like they are busy.*

Uh . . . Aminata can talk to you about the price outside.

Aminata (*mouths*)   NO! No!

Vanessa   Why I gotta go outside? It's madd hot.

Marie   Oh, that's just our policy. We don't discuss the price in the shop.

Vanessa   So I gotta go out in the heat?

Marie   It'll only be for a minute.

Vanessa   Why you can't just tell me now?

Marie   She will. As soon as you step outside . . . Aminata?

Aminata *smiles weirdly at* **Vanessa**.

Vanessa   Ummm, why you looking like that? (*To* **Marie**.)

Why she looking like that? I don't need nobody touching my hair who got an attitude.

Marie   No no. It's fine. She's fine. Right?

Aminata   Yeah, I'm fine. Come. We won't be outside long. I know it's hot.

Vanessa   Oh my God. All this just to say a stupid price. Like . . .

She walks out of the shop and **Aminata** *follows behind.*

Bea   Hmph. These people.

Ndidi (*to* **Chrissy**)   Okay, how is it now?

Chrissy   Yaaasss! Perfect.

(*Looks in mirror excitedly.*) "Okay, ladies now let's get in formation!" (*Fishes money out of purse.*) Here you go. Thank you so much.

Ndidi   You're welcome.

Chrissy   You got a card?

Ndidi   I do.

She pulls one from her station.

Here you are.

Chrissy   Thank you. I'll definitely come back. What days are you here? I have to tell my friend to come. She's been looking for a new hair-braiding lady.

Bea   Oh, well here's my card. Tell your friend that I can do her hair nice-nice. And you too. I'll do it for cheaper than she does.

Chrissy   Oh great. Even better. Alright cool. Thank you.

Ndidi   You're welcome.   **Bea**   You're welcome!

Bea (*to* **Ndidi**)   And *that's* how you do business.

Chrissy *exits as* **Bea** *smiles at* **Ndidi** *sarcastically.* **Vanessa** *and* **Aminata** *re-enter.*

Vanessa   All that just to talk about a price? Anyway, is this your chair?

Aminata   Yes. Please have a seat.

Vanessa *inspects the seat curiously before she sits down.*

Vanessa   Ugh, what is that smell? And why this seat all warm?!

Aminata   I was just sitting in it.

Vanessa   Okay, well, I ain't tryna sit in nobody's funk. 'Cause some of y'all don't be using deodorant and be bathing out of buckets and shit.

Aminata   I showered today. Just like everyone in here. You have no need to worry.

Vanessa (*sucks teeth*)   Whatever.

Aminata *rolls her eyes out of view of* **Vanessa** *and turns to* **Marie**.

Aminata   Marie, can I get 56 inches in number 4?

Marie   Sure.

She goes to the back closet to get the hair. **Aminata** *steels herself, pulls out a comb from the tube of combs soaking in the bright blue barbicide cleaning fluid, and attempts to start combing through* **Vanessa**'s *hair, but* **Vanessa** *snaps her head away.*

Vanessa   UH UH! I don't know where that comb has been! Here. I got my own comb, brush, oil, and gel. You need to ONLY use these on my hair.

Aminata   Okay.

Vanessa   And don't be combing it all hard.

Aminata   No problem.

She pours some oil into her hands and lightly rubs it through **Vanessa***'s hair.*

Vanessa   OH MY GOD! What are you doing? That's too much oil. You want me to break out?

Aminata   I didn't put too much.

Vanessa   It feels like you poured the whole bottle. It's hella expensive and I don't need you wasting it.

Aminata   Sorry.

Bea (*to herself*)   Sha! Could not be me.

Marie *brings out the packs of hair for* **Aminata***.*

Aminata   Thank you, Marie.

Vanessa   Umm, can I see the pack please?

Aminata *holds the pack up for* **Vanessa***. There is a bit of a struggle as* **Vanessa** *grabs the pack to inspect it.*

(*Barely inspects it.*) Yeah, aight. That's good. 'Cause sometimes folks be tryna use the cheap shit and that will damage your hair.

Marie   Oh no. My mother selects this hair herself.

Vanessa   Your muvah?

Marie   Yes, she owns this shop. And she has a direct source in both China and Malaysia.

Vanessa (*not impressed*)   Okay.

Aminata *starts to part* **Vanessa***'s hair.*

Vanessa   And can you not make the parts too big?

Aminata   Sure. No problem.

Vanessa   And please don't be braiding all tight. I'm not tryna lose all my damn hair or my edges.

Aminata   I don't braid tight. It's fine.

Vanessa   You better not.

(*Sucks teeth.*) Ugh, I'm so tired today.

She puts her headphones on and immediately falls asleep. Everyone looks around confused. **Aminata** *is shocked yet relieved.*

Miriam   Maybe she should have put those on when she came in.

Everyone chuckles. The door opens and **Michelle** *enters.*

Bea   Michelle! Aye! It's good to see you.

Michelle (*nervous*)   Hey there . . . Bea . . . You're here . . . On a Tuesday . . .

Bea   Yeah, yeah. I'm working every day now. How have you been?

Michelle   Good. And you?

Bea   Oh, fine, fine. And how is your son? He's what, six now?

Michelle   Seven.

Bea   Oh my goodness. Time is flying, eh? I remember when you would bring him in here when he was two or three years. He would sit there quiet and read his books or watch his cartoons on the iPad. Such a good boy.

Michelle   Yeah, he's a good one. I got lucky.

Bea   You sure did. Well, I wasn't expecting you today. But my chair is free. I don't have someone coming until three or so. Do you want the usual? Come, sit.

She dusts off her chair, but **Michelle** *hesitates.*

Michelle   Oh no. I uh, actually, um . . . well I was meeting a . . . friend and she told me to meet her here, but I think I wrote the address wrong. Let me call her.

Bea   You know what? She probably lives upstairs. There are some apartments above us you know.

Michelle   Yeah . . . that's probably it.

*She dials and is silently hopeful that this will not turn into a thing. After a quick moment, **Ndidi**'s phone starts to ring. She answers, oblivious that **Bea** has already put it together.*

Ndidi   Eh-low?

Michelle *looks at* **Ndidi**. *Everyone knows what's going on.*

Marie   Oh shit. Not again.

Aminata   Oh my goodness . . .

Ndidi   Eh-low? Are you there?

Miriam   Why today? Why?!

Michelle (*meekly waves*)   Hi. I'm Michelle. Your 12 o'clock.

Ndidi   Oh. Ha! Sorry. I'm Ndidi. How are you?

Bea   Are you fucking serious?

Marie   Can we not do this today, please?

Miriam   Eh-eh, Bea, don't start.

Bea (*to* **Ndidi**)   You must really have a death wish, eh? How many of my customers are you going to steal?!

Ndidi   What are you talking about?

Bea   Everyone in here knows that Michelle has been coming to me for YEARS!

Ndidi   And I'm supposed to know that how?

Michelle   Bea. Please, don't be upset. I called her.

Bea   When? When did you call her, eh?!

Michelle   A few days ago.

Bea   Yeah okay! Marie! Call your mother and tell her she needs to come now! I want this girl fired.

Ndidi   Fired?!

Marie   Okay, Bea—I can't do that.

Bea   Fine, then I will call her myself! Because I am not going to tolerate someone coming in here and stealing all of my customers. I know you have been sneaking and going through my Rolodex.

Ndidi   Are you serious? I have customers of my own.

Bea   And no one should be allowed to get a temporary chair when they are stealing customers.

Michelle   Bea! I called her. I promise you.

Bea   For what? Why you no call me? I've been doing your hair for years.

Michelle   I'm sorry. I wouldn't have come if I had known you were going to be here today.

Bea   Oh really?

Michelle   Listen, Bea—you just . . . haven't done as good of a job lately . . . And it has been taking you twice as long to finish and I just . . . you know . . . wanted to try someone new.

Bea   So you're saying I don't know how to do your braids now?

Michelle   I'm saying that I wanted to try someone new.

Bea   Wanted to try someone new . . . Okay that's fine.

Michelle (*to everyone in the shop*)   I'm so sorry about this.

Bea   No, no. You can find someone new. In another shop because you need to leave!

Ndidi   What?

Michelle   Excuse me?

Bea   You heard me!

Marie   You can't do that, Bea. Any paying customer is allowed to stay.

Bea   No! I have been in this shop the longest of anyone here. Including you, Marie!

And no customer who switches braiders in the same shop should be allowed to stay!

Ndidi   Do you hear yourself?

(*Looks around the room.*) Does she hear herself?

Miriam   Bea, please. Have some reason.

Aminata   Come now, sista. You know we can't do that.

Bea   I will call Jaja right now. I know she will agree with me!

Michelle   You know what? I'm just gonna go.

Ndidi   No, no, no, please. Come and sit. I'm doing your hair.

Bea   No you're not!

Marie   Bea, I think you should go and take a walk outside.

Bea (*stunned, very dramatic*)   OH! So now you are putting me on street duty?!

Marie   I didn't say that—

Miriam   —Eh-eh! She didn't say that.

Aminata (*to* **Bea**)   Just relax, eh. You are going to pull up your blood pressure.

Bea (*slightly emotional*)   I have not had to be on street duty flagging down random people for three years, okay! And I am not going to have someone come in here, steal my customers and force me to stand out on the street like some beggar! I have worked too hard, you hear me? I have worked way too hard for that shit!

Beat. **Bea** *tries to recover as she has become more emotional about this than she imagined. Everyone in the shop stares at her. Eventually* **Bea** *grabs her purse and starts to storm out of the shop.*

Aminata   Where are you going?

Bea   Oh, now you care?! Thanks for having my back, Aminata!

She leaves.

Aminata   Bea . . . Bea!

Everyone stares at each other, unsure of what to do or say. Eventually, **Marie** *goes to* **Michelle** *who is on the verge of a panic attack.*

Marie   I am very sorry, Miss Michelle, but please. Ndidi will do a good job on your hair.

Michelle (*traumatized*)   Are you sure?

Ndidi   Yes, please. I am fine. I am not bothered by her. We have not done anything wrong. Come, sit. Please. I'm very sorry about that.

Michelle *takes a beat before finally deciding to sit down.*

Michelle   I just really don't like conflict, you know?

Ndidi   Yeah . . . So, what style would you like?

Michelle (*traumatized*)   Ummm, just some simple cornrows with zigzag parts. Here, I'll show you a picture.

She pulls up a picture on her phone and **Ndidi** *quickly studies it.*

Ndidi   Okay. Beautiful. Don't worry—I'll do it nice-nice for you, yeah?

Ndidi *pulls a comb out from her drawer and starts to comb* **Michelle**'s *hair. The air in the shop is tense and quiet.* **Marie**, *unsure of what to do to lighten the mood, turns up the song playing on the YouTube channel (If you can get the rights, perhaps "Love Nwantiti" by Ckay.)*

Scene Three: 1:45pm

It's pretty quiet in the shop. **Vanessa** *is still asleep in the chair, but* **Aminata** *is nowhere in sight. It seems everyone has taken some sort of break.* **Ndidi** *is just outside of the shop having a cigarette.*

Miriam *continues to braid* **Jennifer***'s hair quietly and it finally looks like she's made some headway.* **Jennifer** *clicks away on her laptop doing her work as she vents to* **Miriam** *about it.*

Jennifer   . . . Well, it's not quite as exciting as you would think since I'm just like a editorial assistant. Lots of tedious work and very little free time. Always scouring the internet trying to find any little piece of information I can get. Or on the phone with someone's friend's, cousin's, half-sister's grandma—begging them for info or a statement. Or reading. Soooo much reading.

Miriam   Oh, I like reading.

Jennifer   I just want to be in the field, you know?

Miriam   Which field?

Jennifer   Like, going out there and actually interviewing people. Getting the real story. Connecting. Just something that feels more satisfying.

Miriam   Like Anderson Cooper?

Jennifer (*laughs*)   Sure. Something like that.

Miriam   I would watch you on CNN. You have nice, kind face.

Jennifer   Well, thank you, but print is more my thing. And I know it'll happen soon, I'm just impatient. But that's probably what two years of annoying grunt work will do to you.

Miriam   I understand. You just have to keep faith.

Jennifer   . . . Yeah.

Small beat.

So, how long have you been braiding hair?

Miriam   Oh, maybe three years. Here in the shop. It is my first professional job.

Jennifer   Oh my goodness, congratulations.

Miriam   Thank you. Yeah, Jaja, the owner of the shop, um, I meet her when I first came. They have this thing—how you say—like African community center, you know? So other Africans who have been here long time can help people who just come, like me. At first I no want to go because I think it only be old people.

They both laugh.

Jennifer   Yeah, 'cause a community center isn't usually a hot spot for the young folks.

Miriam   Exactly. But it was a mix of people. And we all scared and wanting friends because of what president was saying.

Jennifer   Yeah he's . . . yeah.

Miriam   So Jaja was there and she tell me she have hair braiding shop. And I tell her I braid hair all the time back home. I even braid a little girl's hair right there, a quick style, just to show her I'm good.

And she hire me on the spot. I never know you can make money like this just braiding hair. It's not like that back home.

Jennifer   And where is home?

Miriam   Sierra Leone.

Jennifer   Oh okay.

Miriam   You know it?

Jennifer   Yeah I've heard of it. But I've never been there or anything.

Miriam   You go to Africa before?

Jennifer   Yes, actually. In college. I did a study abroad.

Miriam *nods . . . with a hint of judgment.*

Miriam   Mmmm. Let me guess: Kenya? South Africa? Morocco?

Jennifer   South Africa. Yes! How did you know?

Miriam   That is where everyone goes. No one cares about Sierra Leone.

Jennifer   Awww, well, how long has it been since you were back home?

Miriam   Three years. I came here to make some money and try to be American citizen so I can bring my daughter.

Jennifer   Oh, is she back in Sierra Leone?

Miriam   Yes, with my mother.

She stops braiding for a moment and takes out her phone to show **Jennifer** *a picture. Her daughter is the lock screen of her cell phone.*

Miriam   This is her. She turned five a month ago.

Jennifer   Awww, she's beautiful.

Miriam   Thank you.

Jennifer   I bet it must be hard to be away from her.

Miriam   Yeah It is.

Small beat. **Miriam** *continues braiding, but is struck by a small wave of emotion.*

Jennifer (*noticing* **Miriam**'s *teary eyes*)   Awww . . . Are you okay?

Miriam (*wipes away the one tear she let fall*)   I'm sorry. I no mean to cry, but I miss her a lot.

Jennifer   Yeah, I understand.

Miriam   When I was pregnant with her, it was a real surprise. I was married for two years and all that time I didn't get pregnant so I was thinking, you know, maybe God doesn't want me to have baby. And then one day, it happened.

Jennifer   That's what they say. When you stop trying, it just happens.

Miriam   Yeah.

Jennifer   I bet you and your husband were so excited.

Miriam   Uh, yeah. For a while. But then my husband started to get suspicious. Because you know, in his family, the men they have that . . . Eh, I don't know how to say it in English. *Okobo* . . . like . . . he can't have babies. You know?

Jennifer   Oh . . . He's impotent?

Miriam   Yeah. Yeah. That. And you know, my husband—he's not a good husband. He didn't do anything. No job. He's lazy. I have to do everything in the house. So I was not happy, you know? And then one day, I was at the market and I run into my friends from secondary school. And we are talking and laughing and I'm having a good time and they say, "Miriam! You need to come with us tonight. This new singer is having a show on the beach. You have to come!" And I know my husband no want to go because he don't like anything fun.

(*Sucks teeth.*) So I lie to him and tell him I'm going to my sister's house and I go to the show.

Then, this singer gets on stage and his voice is so . . . amazing. I don't know. Me, I never hear anything like it. Then I look close-close and I see that I know him.

Musa. I know him from when I was small. His family lived down the road from me. Aye, but he looked a lot different now!

Jennifer   Oh okay—he was looking good, huh?!

Miriam   Eh heh! So we stay the whole show and after, I go up to him to see if he remember me and you know what? He say my name before I can even call to him!

Jennifer   Okay! Come on, fate!

Miriam   So Musa and me and my friends, we spend almost the whole night together. It was so much fun. The most fun I have in years. And after, Musa drove me home and told me that he wanted to see me again. And I wanted to see him too. So I kissed him. You know, so he knew I was interested.

Jennifer   Oh my goodness, Miriam!

Miriam (*proud of herself*)   I know. But I didn't care! I can't have some joy in my life?! We all deserve it. And I told you, I'm sick of my husband.

So after a few days, I call Musa and we go out. One time then two times then many times and soon, we start to see each other every day. I go to his shows. Or we go to the beach. A restaurant.

Anything. Joy. That's what I was feeling, eh? For the first time. I tell my sister and she say, "Oh no, Miriam! A woman no supposed to act this way and that," but me, I don't care. I don't know what happened to me. I used to be so quiet.

But with Musa, I want to be loud, you know? Hmph . . .

After a time, Musa say he's going on a tour to Europe. He want to take me but we both don't have enough money for papers and visa. And I'm still married. So he goes. And one month after he leaves, I found out I'm pregnant.

Jennifer   Whaaaaaaaa . . .

Miriam   Eh heh. And my husband very excited because he think, "Oh God has blessed us! I'm not *okobo*!" But me, I know he's still *okobo*.

(*Sucks teeth.*) And when my daughter was born and she no look nothing like him, he start to say that he thinks maybe I'm not always at my sister's house like I say. And he call me all of these names and do you know, he raised his hand to me!

Jennifer   Are you serious?

Miriam   Yes! And I say after all these years! No job! So lazy! No fun! You are so brave to try and hit me?! Me, I don't know what came over me because I just raise up and slap him down.

(*Laughs.*) He look so shocked! He start to say that I was a witch. That I'm possessed. He's so stupid. And I know he believe anything. So I start to, eh, how do you say? Like a snake.

(*She hisses.*) "Sss! Sss. Sss! Yeah, I'm a witch! I'm a big witch!" And then his eyes go big and scared and he start to run away.

They both laugh.

Then, I just pack all of my things and I go to my mother's house. She help me get divorce from him which was very hard. It's not like here. Back home, woman not supposed to leave man. So I let him say that I'm a witch and since court feel sorry for him, I get divorce.

But I no care . . . I was free.

Hmph. Then I save money for long time and apply for visa for America. It take me eight times because they no want to give visa to Africans, but I'm lucky. I get approved for America because my cousin live here and have a good job as nurse, you know respectful job, so they approve me. So I leave my daughter and come. But I'm going home soon to visit. And I want to bring my daughter back with me.

Jennifer   Wait, wait, wait, but what happened with Musa? You never spoke to him again?

Miriam (*smiles fondly*)   Musa . . . I talked to him every now and then but we lose touch. He travelled so much. Different phone numbers. And I never keep up. But my friend came into the shop the other day and she say that Musa is back in Sierra Leone. And that he was looking for me. He wants to be with me.

(*Smitten.*) So I'm happy about that.

Jennifer   Are you going to tell him about your daughter?

Miriam   I think so. He say he always want baby with me. So I don't know. Maybe he'll be happy. Maybe he'll come to America and sing. He's really good. He can be like . . . eh, eh . . . Usher. Yeah, Usher. But from Sierra Leone.

They laugh.

Jennifer   Now me thinking you were this shy, quiet lady.

Miriam   You see? I tell you. Everyone think I'm quiet. I'm not like average African woman, eh. No more time for quiet.

I want to be loud, yeah? Yeah. Very loud.

Ndidi *comes back in from her smoke break with* **Michelle**, *whose hair is half braided and is carrying a McDonald's bag. They settle back into their posts.*

Michelle   Thanks for letting me grab something to eat.

Ndidi   No problem.

Michelle (*still nervous from earlier*)   Did I miss anything?

Ndidi (*reassuring*)   No, no. It's quiet in here. For once.

They all chuckle. **Miriam** *smiles to herself.*

Scene Four: 2:30pm

A dramatic scene in a Nollywood film plays on the TV. **Aminata** *is finishing* **Vanessa**'s *hair who is still asleep.* **Miriam** *is still working on* **Jennifer**'s *hair—more progress.* **Ndidi** *is finishing the* *ends of* **Michelle**'s *cornrows.* **Marie** *stands in the middle of the shop holding the broom, as she has stopped sweeping and is now also caught up in the dramatic scene.*

Jennifer   Hey, I think I need to walk around for a little bit.

Miriam   Okay.

Jennifer   I'm gonna go to the store to get a snack. Do you need anything?

Miriam   Oh no, I'm fine. Thank you.

Jennifer *covers her unfinished hair with a scarf and walks out to the shop.*

Ndidi (*re the screen*)   Ooh, ooh, ooh! This is my favorite part.

(*Stands up to perform like "Constance" on the screen.*)

"I see! So you think that you can say whatever you want and I will open my heart back up to you?! Do you think I am some stupid goat on the side of the road? That you can pick me up whenever you want?!"

(*Now she's the male lover, "Richard"; deep voice.*)

"Constance! Has your mind flown out of the window?! What are you saying to me?!"

(*As "Constance."*) "I am saying the words you never want to hear! The truth! And it is clear that the truth is not something your brain can handle!"

(*As "Richard."*) "You say what?! I can handle anything! In the name of God!"

(*As "Constance."*) "Okay, so call God and not me. Because unlike him, I am never going to answer YOUR CALL again!"

The whole shop applauds for **Ndidi** *and her masterful performance.*

Marie   Okay, Ndidi!

Miriam   More like Angela Bassett, o!

Ndidi (*bows, suddenly humble*)   Thank you. Thank you.

Miriam   A woman of many talents. What are you doing here? You need to go to Hollywood!

Ndidi   I did like four or five Nollywood movies back home in Nigeria.

All Women   You did? / Eh eh! Nollywood! / Excuse me?!

Ndidi   Yeah, I like all of those things. Dance. Acting. Music. You see, me, I'm always playing some music.

Marie   I just thought you were trying to block us out.

Ndidi   Sometimes, yes.

She and **Marie** *laugh.*

Michelle   So you didn't want to stay and become a big star?

Ndidi   I don't know about that. Maybe when I go back, I will try again. But me, I'm good with braiding hair too. My mother always said, "If you have skillful hands, they will always be full of money." And I have so many friends who came to America and say that you can make ten times more than what I make back home to braid hair. I didn't believe that until I came here and saw for myself. So now, Nollywood will have to wait, eh.

Marie   I get that.

Ndidi   You know, before my shop burned down, I had JUST worked up to having my own chair. Only had it for three months and then—boom.

Miriam   You were assistant all that time?

Ndidi   Two years. Everyday. "Hey Ndidi—can you finish the rest of these braids? I need to eat. I need to go to the store. I need to pray. I need to, need to, need to." So when the owner started seeing that I was finishing the braids faster than the braider who started it, I said, "Either you give me a chair or I quit."

Marie   And she gave you one fast right?

Ndidi   Chai! Fast-fast! She knew if I walked out, so would half of her money.

The whole shop "mmm's" in agreement.

Michelle   Money talks.

Ndidi   And money can walk too, o!

She and **Michelle** *give each other a high five as they laugh.*

Aminata (*tapping* **Vanessa**)   Hello. You are all done now.

Vanessa (*waking up*)   Huh? Oh, really Wow. I slept through it all?

Aminata   Yes. (*Under breath.*) Thank God.

Vanessa   My fault. I'm so tired. I've been working overnights at the hospital the past two months.

Aminata   It's not easy to work through the night. I've done that before.

Vanessa   Yeah, I be passing out anywhere now. But I'm going on vacation tomorrow. Aruba.

Aminata (*feigns excitement*)   Ohh!

Vanessa   That's why I wanted a good protective style.

Aminata   Yes, well, this will be nice-nice for your vacation. They look good.

Vanessa (*looks in mirror—impressed*)   Yeah, they do. Okay. Alright.

Aminata   Thank you.

She takes the sheen spray and starts to spray **Vanessa**'s *head, but* **Vanessa** *snaps her hand to stop her.*

Vanessa   What are you doing?

Aminata   It's a sheen spray.

Vanessa   I don't want that on my head. I literally told you to only use *my* products on my hair. Like . . .

Aminata (*bites her tongue*)   Sorry.

Vanessa   You know what, let me get outta here. (*Hands her the money.*) Huh.

Aminata   Thank you.

Vanessa   And let me get your card so I can make an appointment next time.

Aminata (*lies*)   Oh . . . I don't have any cards left.

Vanessa   You don't?

Aminata   Yeah . . . no. I ran out—I ran out.

Vanessa   Whatever. Y'all be doing too much in here for me.

Marie   Your hair looks nice.

Vanessa   I know . . .

She exits.

Marie (*smiles sweetly*)   Sorry . . .

Aminata   You will be lucky if I ever talk to you again!

Marie   Well, did you at least get a good price?

Aminata (*proud*)   Of course!

Marie   Then that's all that matters.

Aminata   No, my peace of mind matters!

They both laugh it off. **Olu, The Jewelry Man** *enters the store.*

The Jewelry Man   Afternoon, ladies. Afternoon.

All Women   Afternoon sir. / How are you? / Hello.

The Jewelry Man   I have some nice things for you ladies today. Earrings. Necklace. Rings.

Bracelets. All the nice things. You want?

Miriam   No thank you.

The Jewelry Man   And for you, beautiful Ndidi. How are you?

Ndidi (*smiles, flattered*)   I'm fine, Olu, how are you?

The Jewelry Man   Much better now that I am basking in the light of your smile, o.

Ndidi   Thank you.

He lays down his tray of goods to pull something out of his book bag.

The Jewelry Man   Here. I have something for you. Last time I was here, you mentioned you wanted some large hoops. So I went and had these made for you. They are even dipped in 14 carat gold—since I know you have sensitive skin.

Ndidi (*moved*)   Really?

The Jewelry Man   Of course.

Ndidi   These are beautiful.

The Jewelry Man   For you? Only the best.

*A young woman, **Radia**, walks into the shop.*

Marie   Hi. Welcome. Can I help you?

Radia *barely looks up from texting on her phone.* **Marie** *recognizes her, but is not sure what to do.*

Radia   Yeah, hi. I actually wanted to make an appointment for tomorrow afternoon to get some braids.

(*Looks up, finally.*) What times do you have available? Wait . . . Kelly?

Marie   Radia . . . Hi.

They hug.

Radia   Hi. Oh my God. What are you doing here? Wait, you work here?

Marie   Umm, yeah, I do. This is actually my mom's shop.

Radia   Oh wow. Small world.

Marie   Yeah . . . it is.

Radia   So you're working here until you start school?

Marie   Something like that.

Radia   Yeah, me too. My dad hooked me up with an internship at *Vanity Fair*. It's so crazy. I'm just dressing in designer clothes all day and getting paid.

Marie   That's amazing.

Radia   Yeah, it's cool. And my dad is all, (*mimics father*) "Now this will definitely look good on your resume when you start at Dartmouth."

You know how our parents can be. It's always about "being the best."

Marie   I know, right.

Radia   Speaking of schools—did you ever decide where you were going to go?

Marie   Oh, I um . . . decided to take a gap year. Just to you know, give myself a little break.

Radia   Okay! On your Malia Obama flow. I feel that.

Marie   Something like that.

Radia   Well, no doubt you'll end up going wherever you want Ms. Valedictorian. I'm still lightweight mad I missed it by like half a percentage.

Radia *laughs and* **Marie** *joins her, but it's clearly fake.*

Marie   Yeah, sorry about that. Anyways, so you wanted to book an appointment?

Radia   Yeah, I'm going to Milan for a few days as part of my internship and I want to get my braids done before I go. You know? Just to have something easier to manage.

Marie   Italy . . . wow. That sounds amazing.

Radia   It is! You ever been?

Marie   Uh, no. But it's on my bucket list!

Radia   Oh my God, Kelly! We should all plan a trip next year! You would love it—the food is so amazing. We should totally have a little AP Lit class reunion.

Marie   Yeah . . . That would be amazing. (*Wants this to end.*)

Anyways, so yeah, I'll schedule you for tomorrow at 2pm—does that work?

You'll be with Miriam—she's great.

Radia (*plugs it into her cell phone*)   Perfect. Thank you . . . Oh my God! It was so good running into you! I like never come to Harlem, but I really need to. It's so cute up here.

Marie   It is . . . Yeah.

Radia   Anyways . . . Well, if you're working tomorrow, I'll see you then.

Marie   Okay. Bye!

Radia   Bye!

She exits. **Marie** *is relieved that that dagger-filled exchange is over.* **Aminata** *saunters over to* **Marie**.

Aminata   Marie . . . who is "Kelly"?

Marie   "Kelly" is who everyone at school thinks I am.

Aminata   Oh! So you're still using your cousin's papers? For how long now?

Marie   I don't know, Aminata. Another thing my mom is still working on.

Aminata *makes a face—she won't push it.* **Bea** *walks into the shop. The whole place falls silent for a moment—it's clear she is still in a mood.* **Ndidi** *clocks* **Bea***, but continues to browse* **Olu'***s earrings. She puts her purse down, goes to the closet to grab packs of hair for her next customer, and sits at her station to sort it.*

Aminata (*eventually*)   Are you okay?

Bea   Yeah.

Aminata   I would have gone to look for you if I didn't have a customer.

Bea   It's fine. I just ran a few errands.

Aminata   Okay . . .

(*Small beat.*) You know you can take the day if you want. I don't think it's going to be as busy today.

Bea   No it's fine. I have a customer coming in a few minutes. Or at least I hope she stays my customer.

Michelle *tenses up again.* **Ndidi** *hears that jab, but continues to look through* **Olu'***s jewelry selection while braiding.*

Ndidi   Here. I'll take these two. How much?

The Jewelry Man   It's on the house.

Ndidi   Eh-eh. Olu, please. No. This is your business. Let me pay. I insist.

The Jewelry Man   No, no. It's fine. I promise.

Ndidi   Yeah?

The Jewelry Man   It is my sincere pleasure.

Ndidi   Thank you.

The Jewelry Man   And next time, I'll show you some of my new rings. I want to get a head start on knowing what you like, eh For the future.

Ndidi (*giggle flirt*)   You are so foolish.

The Jewelry Man   You ladies have a good afternoon.

He exits.

Everyone (*like school children*)   Oooohhhhh.

Miriam   Ah-ah! So are you hurting?

Ndidi   From what?

Miriam   From how hard you've fallen in love?!

Everyone   Ayyyyyeee!

Ndidi (*to* **Michelle**)   Okay. You're all done here.

Michelle (*looking in mirror*)   Thank you so much, Ndidi.

Ndidi   No problem.

Michelle   This is perfect. It's my family reunion this weekend and I really didn't want to worry about my hair.

Ndidi   I understand.

Bea *clears her throat loudly.* **Michelle** *tenses again as she walks towards her.*

Michelle   And Bea, again, I'm so sorry about all of this. I just, you know . . . Anyway, I'm sorry.

Bea (*dismissive*)   It's fine.

Michelle   Okay.

(*To* **Ndidi**.) And Ndidi—I'll call you in a few weeks. (*Whispers.*) When you're back at your . . . other . . . yeah, okay. Bye!

Michelle *exits. The movie continues to play filling up the silence.*

Bea   And what nonsense are we watching now?

Aminata   Oh this is a good one. You'd like it.

Bea   Doubt it . . . Ugh, what is that smell? Is that you?

Aminata   What?

Bea   What are you eating?

Aminata   It's just rice and fish stew.

Bea   Mmph. I don't know if I would eat that if I were you. It smells like it's gone bad.

Aminata *is not sure what to make of this shift.* **Bea** *is just being a petty mean girl.*

Aminata   Ummm no it's fresh. I just got it at the store yesterday.

Bea   You see. And when I get my shop, there won't be any eating of smelly foods like this. You don't see how it's stinking up the whole shop?

Aminata   We always eat whatever we want in here.

Bea (*laughs*)   No, YOU always do that. And you like to get food from that dirty market.

No surprise. Nothing but bush people in there anyway.

Jennifer *re-enters.*

Jennifer (*to* **Miriam**)   I got you some tea. I know you said you didn't want anything, but I couldn't not get you something. You're working so hard.

Miriam   Oh thank you. I appreciate that.

Sheila, *who is talking on the phone, loudly, enters.*

Sheila (*on the phone*)   I KNOW, RIGHT?! GIRL! I COULDN'T BELIEVE IT. LIKE, DIDN'T WE TELL JONATHAN THAT IF HE DIDN'T FIX HIS PRESENTATION, NO ONE WOULD GET ON BOARD WITH THE P.W.M ACQUISITION?! THANK YOU! THANK YOU! HOLD ON. HOLD ON A SECOND.

(*Normal volume.*) Hey, sis. Do you have anyone free who can do a sew-in for me?

Marie   Oh yeah, sure. Ummm . . . Ndidi can do it for you.

Bea *sucks her teeth extra-loud.*

Sheila   Thank you so much. Oh, bathroom?

Marie   Right in the back there.

Sheila   Thanks.

(*Back in phone.*) AND THAT'S EXACTLY WHY I DIDN'T WANT PATRICIA TO BE ON THAT ACCOUNT. IT'S VERY CLEAR THAT SHE'S STUPID! YOU KNOW I'M RIGHT!

(*Offstage/in the bathroom.*) OKAY, WELL, HANG IN THERE, GIRL I'LL SEE YOU TOMORROW! BYE!

James *enters the shop. All of the women look at him and immediately roll their eyes. He walks in, ever so confident, and smiles a megawatt smile at everyone despite their non-excitement to see him. You can tell immediately this is a man who is truly in love with himself.*

James   Ladies! . . . Good afternoon.

All Women (*over it*)   Hi James / Hey / Whatever.

James   All of you are looking beautiful as always.

Miriam (*doesn't look up from braiding*)   Mmph.

Bea (*sucks teeth*)   This guy.

James *walks over to* **Aminata**, *but she is not excited to see him.*

James   Hi, darling.

Aminata   Why are you here? Are you trying to ruin my day?

James   Don't be like that, my love. I was just trying to surprise you, eh?

Aminata   You surprise what?!

James (*hands her a plant*)   Here. I got this for you. A rare African violet. For my African Queen.

Aminata *tosses the plant. The whole shop sucks their teeth and/or laughs at* **James. Sheila** *returns from the bathroom and sits in* **Ndidi***'s chair.*

Aminata (*unimpressed*)   Thank you. Is that all?

James   Ah ahn! Still giving me cold shoulders?

Aminata   You're lucky that's all it is.

James (*laughs*)   Look at you. Jokes. You are so silly, Ami.

Aminata   James, I am not playing with you. I told you to give me some space. I need time to think.

James   Of what? More foolish reasons you will make up in your head for why we cannot be together?

Aminata   No, because I don't need any more reasons.

Miriam (*under her breath*)   Exactly!

James   Ami. Come now. She was just a friend. Her father passed away back home and she came over for some consoling. I'm telling you. What you saw was just a hug. Nothing else.

Aminata   You know? If this was the first time, maybe I could believe you. But how many women do you need to hug, eh? And how many times am I supposed to believe that they are all just friends? You have a new "friend" every month!

James   Oh, okay. So you don't know how to leave things in the past? You see. You just want to make problems for nothing.

Aminata   I'm making problems? And what would you say if you came in here and saw me hugging another man?

James Well, that's silly. Why would you be doing that at work? You're supposed to be braiding hair.

Aminata And you're not supposed to bring other women into our . . . excuse me, MY house! And what about Essa? This is the example that you want to set for your son?!

James *smirks. He's sliding into his usual manipulative tactics. A master of gaslighting.*

James Look at this. Look at you. Getting all upset. Making your blood pressure high. For what? You know that is dangerous for you, yeah?

Aminata I want my keys back, James!

James Are you serious?

Aminata Are YOU serious?

James Ah! Ami. Ami. Ami. Please. I don't want to do this with you. I love you too much for this.

Aminata James—

James —Woman! You are all I think about. Look at me. Giving you plants. Always thinking, always searching, always trying to find new ways to show you my heart. But it's not easy, eh. It is not easy to find new ways to tell you what your love means to me.

Bea (*eyes roll*) Sha!

James I'm telling you the truth, now. There is no one else for me, Aminata. Only you. And if I'm lying, may God strike me down right now.

All the women casually take a step away from him.

(*Looks up at the ceiling, winks and smiles.*) You see? I'm still here. (*Playful.*) I'm still here, oh. You are not getting rid of me that easily, baby!

Aminata *laughs. The charm of this man. It's working.*

Aminata   Whatever.

James   Listen, let's discuss this when you get off today, eh?

We'll go and get beef patties from the place you like and we'll talk it all out, yeah?

Aminata (*weakening*)   I don't know . . .

James   Come now. You know that sounds good. Especially after a long day at work.

Aminata (*softly*)   Okay.

James   Yeah?

Aminata   Yeah.

James (*smiles and leans in closer*)   Yeah?

Aminata   Eh, I said yeah.

James *laughs and gives* **Aminata** *a kiss and she melts. She's suddenly a teenager again.*

James   There's my smile.

Aminata   No, it's my smile.

James   Okay, it can be yours. But let me borrow it from time to time, yeah?

Aminata   You are so silly. Get out of here.

James   I'll see you later.

Aminata   Yeah, fine.

James *starts to walk out, but turns back around.*

James   Oh, I almost forgot. I wasn't able to make it to the bank today to get out cash. Do you have any I can hold until later?

Aminata (*pulls money from her pocket*)   Yeah . . . sure.

James   I don't need much. Just a couple hundred.

Aminata *hands* **James** *some money.*

James   Thank you, baby.

He kisses her on the cheek one last time. The whole salon sucks their teeth.

(*Laughing.*) Don't be jealous, ladies.

Bea   Trust me. We're not.

James   Ah, Bea.

Bea   James.

James   I know you are the main one filling my wife's head up with your nonsense.

Bea   How would you know what I'm doing? Maybe if you had a job, you wouldn't have so much time to think.

Aminata   Bea . . . please.

Bea   I'm just saying what we're all thinking.

James   But you're the only one talking.

Bea   Because I actually have something to say.

James   Tell me, Bea—where is your husband? Oh that's right, you don't have one.

Because all four of the men you married ran for the hills.

Bea   Wow.

(*To* **Aminata**.) I see how much you like to talk, Ami.

James   Listen, if you want to be mean and lonely, don't bring other people down there with you, yeah?

Bea *doesn't have a retort to that sting.* **James** *walks to the door.*

James (*to* **Aminata**)   I'll see you later darling. (*Blows a kiss.*)

He exits.

Aminata   Hey listen, Bea—

Bea   —He missed going to the bank? It's the middle of the afternoon.

Aminata (*sucks teeth*)   Excuse me? You need to mind your business, alright?

Bea   Then stop bringing your business in here.

Aminata   Oh really?! You are one to judge.

Bea   Hey! Don't turn this on me. I'm just trying to be a good friend to you! Even though, clearly you don't know the true meaning of that!

Aminata   Oh this is friendship to you? Telling me what to do? Throwing insults? You don't have to worry about me. I've kicked James out!

Bea   That's great! So now let's sort out how many times you are going to let him back in?

Sheila (*chortles*)   Oop! Okay.

Some of the women in the shop look around at each other: "Damn that's harsh."

Aminata   Whatever, Bea! You don't know the first thing about real love.

Bea   Oh, I don't?

Aminata   No, you don't! Anyone who makes one little mistake, that's it! You're done with them.

Bea   Well, pardon me that I don't like to sit around and get taken advantage of for fun! Are you that desperate for a man?!

Miriam   Eh, Bea!

Marie   Okay, ladies . . . can we . . . just . . .

Aminata *stares at* **Bea**.

Aminata   You know, all this time, when you talk about how your family back home won't speak to you—I would think

"How?! How could they not want anything to do with their own flesh and blood?!" But now. Hmph. Now, I understand!

She grabs her bag.

(*To* **Marie**.) I'm going to pick up Essa from school and bring him to my sister's place. I'll be back soon.

Marie Sure.

Aminata *exits.*

Bea (*to* **Marie**)   Look at the kind of shop your mother is running. Hmph! Look at the people she hires. Just wait until I get my own shop. Professionals. Nothing but professionals. None of this drama nonsense.

Scene Five: 4pm

The shop is bustling. **Miriam** *is still working on* **Jennifer**'s *hair and it looks like it is almost done.* **Ndidi** *is still styling* **Sheila**'s *hair.* **Bea** *is braiding a new customer,* **Laniece**, *who is eating a large meal.*

Aminata *runs in full of excitement.*

Aminata   Guess what?!

All Women   What?

Aminata   I WON THE SCRATCH-OFF!

All Women   AYE! / Congrats! / Look at you!

Aminata (*starts to dance*)   It's a celebration, o! Come! Celebrate me and my riches now! Come, Miriam!

Come, Marie! Even you too, Ndidi! Come, come, come!

Marie *turns up the music playing on the YouTube channel. (If you can get the rights, perhaps "Come and See My Moda" by MzVee and Yemi Alade.)* **Aminata** *starts to get down in the middle of the shop and all of the women, except* **Bea**, *join her as they hype her up.*

All Women   Aye! Go, Ami! / You betta dance, oh! / Go 'head, sis! / AYYYYYE!

Laniece   Wait, wait, wait—so how much did you win?

Aminata   Two fifty!

Miriam   Aye! Two hundred and fifty thousand?!

Aminata   No! Two hundred and fifty dollars! But money is money, o!

Aminata *is in the middle of her own little nightclub she's now created with the other braiders in the shop.* **Miriam** *goes up to* **Bea**.

Miriam   Come, Bea! Join us. You know that you want to dance. Come now!

Bea   I'm fine.

Miriam   Come on! Go, Bea! Go Bea! Go, Bea!

Marie *joins* **Miriam** *as they push* **Bea** *towards the center of the shop.*

Miriam *and* **Marie**   Go, Bea! Go, Bea! Go, Bea! Go, Bea!   **Laniece**   Okay, Bea! I see you too!

Bea *cracks a smile, stands, and does a quick little dance, before she laughs and waves everyone off.* **Jaja** *enters. She is dressed in an extravagant all-white African wedding gown. She looks incredible.*

All Women   JAJA! AYYYYEEE!

All the women send their cheers to **Jaja** *as she enters this party happening in her shop.*

She dances into the middle of the floor and some women even playfully shower her with dollars—African wedding style. She dances until she is winded, but everyone in the shop applauds her. **Marie** *turns down the music.*

Aminata   AYE! Jaja! Look at you, eh? Beautiful! Just beautiful.

Jaja   Oh, this old thing.

The women laugh.

Eh, Marie, get me some water.

Marie   Yes, Mommy.

Jaja   But listen, eh, I don't pay you all to dance around and party now. Are we making money today or what?

Miriam/Ndidi/Aminata   Of course we are. / Yes! / You know it.

Jaja *walks over to* **Jennifer** *and inspects* **Miriam***'s work.*

Jaja   Eh, Miriam. Nice job. You have such a good steady hand.

Miriam   Thank you, sista.

Jaja (*leans over to* **Jennifer**) And you have a lot of patience. Your boom boom must be hurting, yeah?

Jennifer (*laughs*)   A little bit.

Jaja   You can get up and stretch anytime you want.

Jennifer   Thanks, I definitely have.

Jaja   She's almost done—won't be too long.

Jennifer   That's . . . what I keep hoping.

Jaja *saunters over to* **Bea**.

Jaja   Aye, Sista Bea. How are you?

Bea (*curt*)   I'm fine.

Jaja (*mimics her*)   "I'm fine."

(*Laughs.*) Since when are you this quiet? Did someone die?

Bea (*weak laugh*)   No. I'm just . . . working.

Jaja *catches eyes with the rest of the shop. She gets that* **Bea** *is in a mood and leaves it alone.*

Jaja   Okay . . . I'll let you keep working.

Ndidi   You look very nice, Jaja.

Jaja   Oh, thank you, my dear.

Ndidi   Are you excited?

Jaja   Beyond. You know how long I have been waiting for this? Sha! Longer than you've been alive.

Ndidi *and* **Jaja** *laugh.*

Aminata   And where is Steven now?

Jaja   He's on his way to come and get me. I told him that I needed to come to the shop first to show off. Make you all jealous.

Bea   Mmmm . . .   **All Women**   Ayyyyye!

Jaja   Listen, this was made special by that Gambian woman. You know, with the store on 116th. I told her "make it nice-nice. This will be my last dress as an African and my first as an American, o!" Ayyye!

All Women   Ayyyye!

Jaja   I'm telling you, ladies. This is it. This is the life that God planned for me, you know? Get all of this nonsense immigration stuff out of the way so I can really make a name for myself here.

Miriam   That's right.

Aminata   That's the only way.

Jaja   'Cause these people, hmmm. I have been running this shop for ten years. Hurting my back, arthritis in my hands. Paying all of this money to this landlord for what? All for them to raise the rent whenever they feel like it. Always making sure to keep us under their foot. And now, these people are making it hard for my baby to go to college.

Marie   —Mom. Can we not—

Jaja   —After allll the money I spent sending her to private school. No one said anything then. They were happy to take my money. And taxes too! How is that fair, eh? If we are paying taxes, then we should become citizens, that's it!

Ndidi   I agree.

Jaja   And you know they are all jealous of her, eh? 'Cause she's smarter than most of their children! So now all of a sudden, they have all of these questions: "Oh let me see her birth certificate please." "When did you all come here?" "Where did she go to school in Senegal?" Jealous! You hear me?

Marie   That has nothing to do with it, Mom. How long am I supposed to use the I.D. of some "cousin" I've never even met?!

Jaja (*deflects*)   They are just trying to keep you down! That is all it is. Even now, they are trying to say, "Oh she needs to pay ten thousand dollars so she can apply for a 'dream'"! What kind of nonsense is this?

Marie   Well, it doesn't matter. It's not like we can afford it anyway.

Jaja   But who can? What kind of perfect immigrant are they looking for, eh? When it comes to us, the rules are alllllways changing!

Aminata   That's the problem.

Jaja   Exactly! This country is fine with TAKING. They are even fine with us GIVING, but the moment we ASK for something? Hey! That's it. Who are you? Dirty Africans! Get out of our country!

Go back to your . . . "shat-holes."

The whole shop does collective teeth sucks and hisses.

Okay, so you want me to go? Fine, I will go. But when do you want me to leave? Before or after I raise your children? Or clean your house? Or cook your food? Or braid your hair so you look nice-nice before you go on your beach vacation?!

(*Mimics a white woman customer.*) "Oh please, miss. Can you give me the Bo Derek hair please?"

The whole shop laughs in agreement.

So now that's it. Today, I will be on THEIR level. When they ask me to go back to my country, I will just—(*She turns in place.*) Okay, I'm here—in my country!

Jaja *and the rest of the shop laugh.*

Miriam   Jaja, you are too much oh.

Jaja   I know.

Walks over to **Marie***.*

Jaja   And then my little baby girl here. We will make her a citizen too, yeah. And she'll go to university. And become a doctor. And buy me a four-storey Brownstone on Lenox Ave, yeah!

Marie   Mom. Please.

Jaja   Okay, you don't have to be a doctor. I'll take engineer.

She laughs.

Miriam   You have to let her be what she wants, Jaja.

Jaja   I'm just playing with her. She can be whatever she wants. This is America after all.

(*To* **Marie***.*) Oh my goodness—just smile, Marie. For once, everything is working out for us.

Marie   Working out for you maybe . . .

Jaja *playfully rolls her eyes at* **Marie***'s attitude.*

Jaja   You all see this? That's how I know she's American. You see how she's talking to her mother? She won't even come to the courthouse with me. She says: (*Mimics daughter—bad New York accent.*) "I don't support what you're doing, Moooom. I don't like him for you, Moooom. How do you know you can trust him, Mooooom?"

(*Laughs.*) Because she needs to approve something for me.

(*To* **Marie**.) I'm the mother here, yeah?

Marie (*trying to be respectful*)   I know that, Mommy. I just don't want to go and watch you marry someone I don't like.

Jaja   Okay, that's fine. But you're going to have to get over that because he's going to be your new father.

Marie   Yeah . . .

Jaja   You don't have to approve, but you have to respect. And anyway, aren't you happy that I don't have to be worried about us being sent back? He cares about us.

Ah, You just worry too much. And it's all for nothing. You're going to give yourself wrinkles. You'll be looking older than every woman in this shop!

She laughs as she kisses **Marie** *on the forehead. A horn honks outside.*

Jaja   Ah, that must be *Steven*. I've got to go. We don't have time to waste, eh.

Miriam   Oh, did you end up finding a witness?

Jaja   Yes, one of Steve's friends. And he's a white too, so we're going to be just fine.

Aminata   Oh, why? They don't believe Steven is with you?

Jaja   No, darling. They can't believe I am with HIM!

Everyone in the shop laughs, except **Bea**.

Jaja   Alright, Marie . . . I'll see you later, yeah? I'll bring you some cake.

Marie   Oooh, that pound cake from Cleo's?

Jaja   You know it.

Laniece   Awwww . . . I love Cleo's.

Marie (*to* **Laniece**)   Right?

Jaja   Okay, let me go now. The next time you ladies see me, I will be Mrs. Jaja . . . Jacobson!

The shop erupts with a chorus of "Ayyyyyye! Mrs. Jacobson!"

Aminata   Bye, Jaja! See you soon.   **Ndidi**   Good luck!

Miriam   See you later, Jaja.   **Marie**   Bye, Mom.

Jaja *waves and exits the shop.* **Marie** *stares out of the door at her mother. A new song comes on the playlist. (If you can get the rights, perhaps "Fall" by Davido.)* **Aminata** *jumps up.*

Aminata   Aye! This is it. This is the song! Look at this. Now it's really a celebration. Marie, come, come. Give everybody a cup, yeah?

Marie *is confused, but she grabs a bunch of cups from the water cooler and hands them out.* **Aminata** *goes under her station and starts digging.*

Miriam   What are you doing, Ami?

Aminata   I only sip from this on very special occasions. Because you know, my doctor. And my "pressure."

Marie   Oh . . . Aminata, I'm only eighteen.

Aminata   Nonsense. Me, I don't care. You will drink.

She pulls out a giant three-liter of orange soda. They all laugh.

I should be watching my sugar, but today? We celebrate.

She quickly pours a little bit for everyone in the shop. They all lift their paper cups in the air.

To Jaja. For building this shop. For letting us all work here. And for giving us all a little bit of hope today, eh? Cheers.

All Women   Cheers.

Marie *takes the remote and turns up the music. They all have caught the bug of happiness and dance. It is joyous and hopeful.*

Scene Six: 9pm

It is the end of the day and the sun has finally set. **Ndidi** *is cleaning up her station.* **Marie** *is counting money.* **Aminata** *is wiping down her chair with a little too much alcohol spray.* **Miriam** *sprays oil sheen on* **Jennifer**'s *head.*

Miriam   Okay. All done. The whole salon applauds.

Jennifer   Wow, we actually made it. (*Laughs.*) Thank you so much. They look beautiful.

Ndidi   Mmm hmm. Very nice.

Jennifer (*pulls money from purse*)   Here you go . . . Now, I threw in a little extra . . .

Miriam *quickly counts the money and realizes that* **Jennifer** *gave her a big tip.*

Miriam   Oh my goodness. Thank you so much.

Jennifer   Make sure you get a nice outfit before you see Musa.

Miriam (*smiles*)   I will.

Jennifer   Alright, well thank you, ladies. I feel like I moved in for the day.

Marie   You did.

They all laugh.

Take care. And please come back again.

Jennifer   Of course. And hey, congrats to your mom.

Marie   Oh, thank you.

Jennifer   Goodnight.

Aminata/Ndidi/Miriam   Night. / Good night! / Get home safe.

Jennifer *exits.*

Ndidi   Alright, I think I'm going to head out too. Unless you need help with something, Marie?

Marie   Oh, no no. I'm fine. I'm going to finish counting and cleaning up and then I'll be on my way.

Ndidi   Fine-fine. I'll see you tomorrow. And Bea, again, I'm sorry about earlier.

Bea (*still has an attitude*)   It's fine.

Everyone stealthily rolls their eyes at each other.

Ndidi   Alright, goodnight, ladies.

Everyone   Bye bye. / Night. / Goodnight.

Ndidi *exits.* **Miriam** *hands* **Marie** *some money.*

Miriam   Here you go. My cut for the day.

Marie   Thank you.

(*Looks curiously at her hands.*) Eh, Miriam. Your fingers are all blistered.

Miriam (*eye roll*)   I know. At least they didn't bleed this time. It's fine. I'll soak them when I get home.

Aminata   Ah ahn! You need to do it now before your whole hand swells up. Trust me. It has happened to me too many times.

Marie   Here, let me get a bowl. We have some Epsom salts in the back.

Miriam   It's not that serious.

Aminata   No, no. You sit down. Marie—go get the stuff.

Marie *exits into the back room.*

Miriam   Oh my goodness—ladies, please.

Aminata   Listen, take it from me. Better you deal with this now before you wake up tomorrow and your hands are so swollen and tight, you won't even be able to hold your toothbrush. Aye! This job.

Sometimes I can't believe I still have fingers.

Eric, The DVD Man *enters the shop with a large bag full of counterfeit DVDs.*

Bea   Hey, my friend. You're a bit late today. We are about to close up.

The DVD Man   Eh. I know sista. I am looking for Marie. Is she still here?

Aminata   Yeah, she's in the back.

Ndidi *comes back into the shop.*

Ndidi   Can you believe I forgot my headphones? How?!

The DVD Man (*worried*)   Oh, dear.

Miriam   What's wrong?

The DVD Man   Oh dear. Aye God. This girl is too young for this.

Bea   What's going on?

Ndidi   Is everything okay?

Marie *re-enters with a bowl and a carton of Epsom salts.*

Marie   Alright, Miriam. Just stick your hands in the bowl and I'll pour in the salts.

(*Notices* **The DVD Man**.) Hey, Eric. How are you?

The DVD Man   Marie, oh Marie. I'm so sorry, o.

Marie   Sorry about what?

The DVD Man *looks at her worried.*

Marie   Eric. What is going on?

The DVD Man   Eh, I have a friend who cleans buildings downtown. She called me just now and say she see all of these police dragging these people and pushing them into vans. She just think they are all criminals. Then she said she seen a woman who look familiar to her. She stopped to look closer and it is the same woman who braid her hair before. Jaja.

All Women   What?

Marie   Are you sure?

The DVD Man   She walked across the street and she see it clear as day. It was Jaja. She say she didn't know Jaja was a criminal but when truck drive away, it say ICE.

Marie   What?

Aminata   Oh my God.

Ndidi   These people!

Marie   Where is she? Do you know where they took her?

The DVD Man   The woman at the front desk say they took them for sham marriage. They are all going to a holding center.

Miriam   Sham marriage? How can they prove that? Jaja and Steven have been together for a long time.

The DVD Man   The woman at the desk tell my friend that he is already married in another state.

Marie *starts to break down.*

Miriam   WHAT?!

Aminata   No.

Ndidi   Wow.

Bea   You see?! I knew it. That man is a criminal!

Marie   Please, do you know where they took her?

The DVD Man   I don't know. My friend say she is going to keep asking but there are so many holding centers.

Aminata   We can call around and see. Miriam, where did Salima say they took her when she got detained?

Miriam   Three different locations. It took us almost a week to find her!

Ndidi   They make it hard on purpose!

Marie (*panicking*)   Oh my God. No. Oh my God.

Aminata   Okay, okay. Let's just relax, eh? It will not take us that long to find her. Don't worry. We will call all of the ones in Manhattan first. Let's look them up.

She goes to her phone.

Marie   And how is that going to help? Even if we do find her, what are we going to do? They aren't going to let her out.

Miriam   Here, let me call my friend. He knows this immigration lawyer. He's very good.

Aminata (*on the phone*)   James. Where are you? I need you to come to the shop as soon as you can. They are saying they took Jaja.

Miriam   Here, Marie. Take down this number. Call the guy right now and ask him what to do.

The DVD Man   Do you want me to call my friend again?

Ndidi   What can I do?

Marie *is trying to breathe. The shop falls silent. No one is sure what to do.*

Aminata   Marie, come. We are going to figure this out.

Marie   How? Figure it out how? Even if we do find her, then what? We can't give them any money. We can't tell them "she's my mother" and they'll let her go free. They might detain me too. And then what? I go back to Senegal? I haven't been there since I was four years old! I don't speak the language. I don't know anyone there. This is the only place I know.

Beat.

I knew this would happen. I knew it. The moment she said that they were going to get married, I knew that something was going to go wrong. I could feel it. Now look. What am I supposed to do? . . .

Bea   Marie, please . . . Your mother cannot do anything with your tears . . . (*To* **The DVD Man**.) Eric, can you see what other information your friend can tell you?

The DVD Man   Yes and I can go downtown myself too. I know some guys who work in that area and they've got some connections. I can see what they know.

Bea   Thank you.

The DVD Man (*to* **Marie**)   Marie, it is going to be fine, yeah?

You—I consider you my sista. And a brother always looks after his sista, okay?

Marie   Thank you, Eric.

The DVD Man   I will check in with you later.

He exits.

Miriam   I'm telling you—you should call that immigration lawyer. I'm sure he can help.

Ndidi   Yes! Call him first thing in the morning.

Marie   The morning. Oh God. She's going to have to stay in there all night.

Aminata   Yes, but hopefully just for the one night.

Marie   I need to get out of here. I need to go pack and find somewhere to stay.

Aminata   What do you mean?

Marie   What if they come looking for me?

Miriam   They are not going to come for you.

Marie   You don't know that.

Aminata   And if they do, so what? They will have to take us all.

Bea   Okay, okay—Come. Here is what we are going to do. We're going to lock up the shop. We're all going to go home with you and pack up all the things you need.

Marie   And where am I supposed to stay?

Bea   With me.

*Everyone looks a bit shocked. Perhaps even **Bea** is shocked at herself.*

Marie   What?

Bea   You will stay with me. I have plenty of room.

Marie   Really?

Bea   Yes. You will stay with me for as long as you need to. And in the morning we will call Miriam's immigration lawyer friend. And Aminata and Ndidi will call all the centers in the city. And we will figure this all out. Together. You are not alone in this.

Jaja is your mother but she could be any of us. And we will fight for her, okay?

Small beat.

Marie   Okay.

Bea   Good . . . Now let's close up.

*The ladies start to close up. They grab their purses, other bags, etc. **Marie** grabs the lock box of money and stuffs it in her bookbag. They quickly clean up and push their chairs back, etc. Each of the ladies step out of the shop. They stand outside of it and stare at each other for a beat.*

Miriam (*eventually*)   Are you hungry?

Aminata   I'm always hungry.

Ndidi   Me too.

Miriam   I can go and get us some Chinese food. Do you want Chinese, Marie?

Marie   Uh, yeah, sure.

Aminata   The usual?

Marie   That's fine.

Ndidi   My treat, yeah? It's the least I can do.

Miriam   Thanks, Ndidi. I'll go and get us a table.

Aminata   I'll go with you.

Ndidi   Me too.

Bea   We'll meet you there.

Miriam   Okay.

Miriam, **Aminata**, *and* **Ndidi** *walk off.* **Marie** *starts to pull the grate down with some assistance from* **Bea**. *She surprises herself with how emotional she becomes as she fumbles with her keys and finally finds the right one to lock up the shop. She stands there for a moment, trying to breathe.* **Bea** *pulls her in for an embrace.*

Bea   Hey. It's all going to be okay.

Marie   But what if it's not?

Bea   Then it's not . . . And after that, it will be okay . . . Listen, you know the one thing that your mother is most proud of?

Marie   What?

Bea   You. Your straight A's. Your valedictorian. How good you are to people . . . Your kindness . . . How you love . . . That's why she wants more for you. To be anything in the world you want to be. Bigger and better dreams than just this shop; which you run better than her . . . But don't tell her I said that.

Marie *softly chuckles.*

Bea   And tomorrow, you'll get up. You'll come here. You'll open the shop. And we will go on. 'Cause as long as the shop is here, so is your mother, yeah? This is Jaja's African Hair Braiding. And we're going to hold onto it for her for as long as we can . . . Sometimes, that's all we can do . . . You understand?

Marie   Yes.

Bea   Good. Now, chin up, eh? We have work to do.

She walks off. **Marie** *stands on the street. She looks to the right and the left. Unsure of what to do. She takes a deep breath and stares up at the awning. The sounds of Harlem on a summer night fill the space as the stage fades to black with only "Jaja's African Hair Braiding" sign remaining illuminated. Fade to black.*

End of play.

For a complete listing of
Methuen Drama titles, visit:
www.bloomsbury.com/drama

Follow us on X and keep up to date with
our news and publications
@MethuenDrama